"Listen to the wise words of a seasoned pastor who knows that being a disciple of Jesus is much more than developing biblical literacy and theological knowledge. Learn how grace embeds your little story in the larger story of redemption and transforms your heart in the process."

> **Paul David Tripp,** President, Paul Tripp Ministries; author, *What Did You Expect? Redeeming the Realities of Marriage*

"Bill has been one the most influential pastors shaping my thinking on discipleship. He brings a holistic, gospel-centered, Jesus-exalting approach to the ongoing formation of the redeemed people of God. I thank God for Bill's impact on my life and I trust that you will as well after reading this book."

> **Jeff Vanderstelt,** Vice President, Acts 29; Pastor, Soma Communities, Tacoma, Washington

"Bill Clem uses his powerful storytelling ability, theological insights, and personal journey to speak straight to the heart of discipleship. Reading this book was like having a cup of coffee with one of the most influential thinkers and ministry leaders of our day."

> **David Livermore,** President, Cultural Intelligence Center; author, *Serving with Eyes Wide Open*

"Through both his writing and his life, Bill Clem has given us an inspiring vision of what it looks like to live out our identity as disciples of Jesus."

> **Pete Kelley,** Lead Pastor, Doxology, Corvallis, Oregon

"Bill Clem shattered all of my preconceptions of discipleship, but in so doing he masterfully painted a beautiful portrait of what a disciple is and what discipleship looks like. A must-read for anyone serious about making gospel-centered disciples."

> **Carlos Montoya,** Lead Pastor, Blaze Christian Fellowship, Santa Fe, New Mexico

"In all my ministry years I have never met anyone who is more adept and passionate about the subject and lifestyle of discipleship. This book will not be one you half read and then set aside for the next garage sale; it will be part of your permanent library, used to equip yourself and others for years to come. In fact, I wager you will read and reread this. It's that good! *Disciple* challenges us all to dig deeper so that we might learn what it means to be a true follower of Jesus and to help others to do the same."

Mike Love, founder, director, Extreme Dream Ministries

"*Disciple* connects the relational community of the triune God to his image bearers in the greatest nonfiction story of all—the story of God. The privilege of playing our part in his story is masterfully told by Clem. Not only is *Disciple* a 'great read'; it is a 'must-study.'"

Mark A. Hoeffner, Executive Director, CB Northwest; Lead Elder, Grace Baptist Church, White Salmon, Washington

Disciple

Other books in Crossway's Re:Lit series:

Community: Taking Your Small Group Off Life Support
by Brad House, 2011

Note to Self: The Discipline of Preaching to Yourself
by Joe Thorn, 2011

*A Meal with Jesus: Discovering Grace, Community, and Mission
around the Table* by Tim Chester, 2011

*Redemption: Freed by Jesus from the Idols We Worship and the
Wounds We Carry* by Mike Wilkerson, 2011

Rid of My Disgrace: Hope and Healing for Victims of Sexual Assault
by Justin and Lindsey Holcomb, 2011

Church Planter: The Man, the Message, the Mission
by Darrin Patrick, 2010

Doctrine: What Christians Believe by Mark Driscoll and
Gerry Breshears, 2010

Leaders Who Last by Dave Kraft, 2010

Scandalous: The Cross and Resurrection of Jesus
by D. A. Carson, 2010

Religion Saves: And Nine Other Misconceptions by Mark Driscoll, 2009

Vintage Church: Timeless Truths and Timely Methods
by Mark Driscoll and Gerry Breshears, 2009

Total Church: A Radical Reshaping around Gospel and Community
by Tim Chester and Steve Timmis, 2008

*Practical Theology for Women: How Knowing God Makes a
Difference in Our Daily Lives* by Wendy Horger Alsup, 2008

Death by Love: Letters from the Cross by Mark Driscoll and
Gerry Breshears, 2008

Vintage Jesus: Timeless Answers to Timely Questions
by Mark Driscoll and Gerry Breshears, 2008

BILL CLEM

DISCIPLE

GETTING YOUR IDENTITY FROM JESUS

FOREWORD BY MARK DRISCOLL

::: CROSSWAY

WHEATON, ILLINOIS

Library of Congress Cataloging-in-Publication Data
Clem, Bill, 1955–
 Disciple : getting your identity from Jesus / Bill Clem ; foreword by Mark Driscoll.
  p. cm.
 Includes bibliographical references and index.
 ISBN 978-1-4335-2349-6 (tp) — ISBN 978-1-4335-2350-2 (pdf)
 ISBN 978-1-4335-2352-6 (ePub)
 ISBN 978-1-4335-2351-9 (mobipocket)
 1. Spiritual formation. I. Title.
BV4511.C54   2011
248.4—dc22   2011007742

Crossway is a publishing ministry of Good News Publishers.

VP		21	20	19	18	17	16	15	14	13	12
14	13	12	11	10	9	8	7	6	5	4	3	2

CONTENTS

FOREWORD

Among Jesus's final words to us—before he returned to heaven after completing his salvation mission—was the command to "make disciples." Subsequently, this is the delight and duty of the Christian church until he returns.

What, though, is a disciple? Whom and how do they worship? What is their identity? Where is their community? What is their mission?

The word *disciple* has been used so often that arguably few people actually spend much time thinking on it deeply and understanding it practically.

Thankfully, our friend and fellow Mars Hill pastor Bill Clem does a masterful job of answering these and other questions about what Jesus intended when he told us to make disciples. His wisdom comes from living as a disciple of Jesus Christ for decades. He has taught literally tens of thousands of leaders of all ages around the nation and world, helped run one of the largest student ministry organizations, led the nation's largest college ministry, served as both a senior and an associate pastor, taught at seminaries, planted a church, and now serves as the campus pastor at our largest Mars Hill campus. He also buried a wife after a long battle with cancer, raised adult children who all love and serve Jesus, and is now a happy grandpa loving a new wife in a new season of life that includes the occasional cigar.

Those of us who know him best will tell you that when the Bible speaks of a loving shepherd, it was referring to Pastor Bill.

We respect him, appreciate him, and enjoy him. He is humble toward other leaders, faithful with Scripture, loving with people, courageous in leadership, flexible in method, and filled with the Holy Spirit.

So, when it came to writing the book on discipleship, we needed him to write it. His work contained in this book serves as the foundation for all of our discipleship at Mars Hill Church and has made a profound difference in people's lives. We are thrilled to share our friend and his wisdom with you.

Mark Driscoll, Senior Pastor,
Mars Hill Church, Seattle

1

THE STORY OF GOD

If you were God, how would you tell a human who you are? *[handwritten: from]* How would you make it plain to people? How would you reveal *[handwritten: explains]* yourself to your own creation? Would you skywrite bullet points such as:

- Eternal
- Infinite
- Wise
- Holy
- Powerful
- Loving

Would you create a cause-and-effect universe in which you insert yourself with interruptions called "miracles"? Would you sign your name on everything and stamp it with "good"? When you think about it, you realize it would not be so easy to disclose yourself to your creation, but God has done so masterfully in a very engaging way.

The Story of God Is Inviting

God has chosen to reveal himself to us through story. *[handwritten: & natural revelation]* We come to know his story in two ways. First, God allows us to see his faithfulness and his patient and providential guidance of the nations. In Exodus 15:11–13, we read about God's people rejoicing over his faithfulness in the drama of Israel's deliverance. Take also, for example, the prophetic oracles of judgment in Isaiah 14–21 against Assyria and Philistia, against Moab, against Damascus, against Egypt, and against Babylon.

Second, he gives us listening privileges into (1) intimate conversations with men such as Moses (in Exodus 32–33 Moses intercedes for the nation as a type of Christ interceding for his people); (2) the promises he makes to Abraham (Genesis 12; 15; and 17 form the basis of the Abrahamic covenant establishing hope throughout the story of God); and (3) the prayers of David (the Psalms are full of emotional laments and humble confessions in David's struggle and that of others to embrace a story line that they, at times, do not enjoy or understand). It doesn't take long to realize that we're not simply hearing a story full of flat characters but one of complexity and dynamic encounters between real persons. This story is fully engaging and involved. One doesn't hear this story without walking away feeling somehow very connected. God's story strikes to our very core because it is a story of persons in relationship to each other.

The God of the Bible does not seem as interested in us knowing *about* him as he desires for us to actually *know* him—to have experiential knowledge of him. (Paul prays that the Ephesians would "know the love of Christ that surpasses knowledge," Eph. 3:19). This experience of coming to know him happens to every person, but in many different ways. One of the primary ways we can come to know him is through the Bible. It contains the story of God's revelation to us. When we read it with this in mind, we are "concerned with God's saving acts and his word as these occur within the history of the people of God."[1] The descriptions and discoveries in the story about God through the lives of those who both know him and oppose him reveal to us a profoundly personal God, one who seeks to be in relationship with his creation.

God tells us his story in engaging and inviting ways so that we will be compelled to become a part of his story. However, throughout history people have tried to make sense of our unique relationship to God in less helpful ways and sometimes in altogether unbiblical ways. Some common analogies of God's relationship to people include copilot, teacher and classroom, primary cause and secondary cause, commander and troops, and hand in glove. Most of us would agree that we don't view our relationship to God in these ways, but it is how some function moment by moment in their relation to God.

Another more helpful and biblical analogy is that of author and characters in a story.[2] God's story is mind-blowing because it is a compellingly real story in which we are all playing a part.

After hearing my presentation in a workshop about the story of God, a man asked if he could talk with me. He disclosed to me his tragic story of abuse and how his brutal stepfather inflicted pain and brokenness into his life and the lives of his siblings. Recently he had been summoned to testify against his abuser in court, which was disturbing, because he thought it was all behind him. All the pain and suppressed memories burst through the dam of emotional containment he had built out of coping skills. In the midst of his pain he had concluded that God hadn't shown up, so he'd check out on God, hermetically sealing within his soul yet another set of unresolved hurts. As I spoke, he sensed his fortress walls giving way, and he began again asking questions such as, "How could God be so uncaring as to script a story line like this for me?" Many people ask similar questions, if not the very same one, every day.

Embracing the servant role of experiencing redemption in God's story rather than abandoning the God of the story because we don't like the way the story is going is perhaps the biggest hurdle to our faith. To place oneself as the character in a story written by another flies in the face of the society and culture in which we live today. The slogan "I am my own master" bellows loudly from both newsstand and blog post. Our world is saturated with the autonomy of the individual, and we simply don't like to think that we are not in complete control of our own destiny.

The man I spoke with was quick to admit that his own parenting style had been shaped for the better by the pain he had experienced and that his quest for a loving God who gives meaning to all that he has made had been heightened through his situation. He just couldn't get to the place of trusting God, because doing so meant that he had no guarantee that God would shield him from further pain. The sad truth is, there is no pain-free life insurance. Whether this man saw himself as the author of his own story or as a cast member in God's story, he still suffered and wanted desperately to know why.

As long as we think we are writing our own story, we will keep adding adventures or characters, thinking that more is the pathway to meaning and happiness. Here's the problem: we just don't have enough resources to get the meaning we crave. Consider the following two scenarios.

Scenario 1. Three drama students have one year left to complete their degrees at private colleges. They estimate their expenses for this final year to be between $125,000 and $175,000. One night they're out shooting pool, and they come up with the idea of creating a play. It seems brilliant, even career savvy. As they start to frame their ideas—script, staging, cast, and venues—they realize that just renting a theater could cost their entire tuition. Undaunted, they scale back and strategize a three-man play they can pull off in a parent's RV storage unit. As they continue to prune back their dream, everyone they talk to—parents, peers, and professors—responds skeptically. All warn the three aspiring actors that starring in a play performed in a garage doesn't have the same potential as did three guys in a garage developing a computer in the 70s. It just can't produce the impact or give the meaning they are hoping for. They will at least need to hire a well-known actor as a draw, which of course is out of the question with their very limited resources.

Scenario 2. A drama student with only a year left to complete her degree auditions for a small part in a Broadway play in New York. She gets a callback and is eventually offered the part. It's not a lead role or anything close to it. But she would be working with some of the best actors, coaches, and producers in the industry—not to mention it's Broadway in New York and a premiere playwriter's script. When this student asks her friends, family, and faculty what they think, they all encourage her to take this once-in-a-lifetime plunge.

What's the difference in the two scenarios? The Broadway play places our student in a world way bigger than herself that involves staging, famous people, promotion—even with a walk-on bit part, she belongs to something huge. The garage players, on the other hand, are on the other side of reality, believing their vision of the way things could be is the way things actually are.

These illustrations are meant to parallel the difference between inviting God into our story (which gives a big-guest appearance to God in a small-time show called "My Life") and being offered whatever role God gives us in his epic drama. Our personal story is actually a distortion of reality and a desire for significance. God's story is reality, and significance can be ours with even a walk-on bit part, because pleasing and glorifying the Creator is the most significant experience offered to created beings.

God reveals himself through the lives of people, and when people realize they are a part of God's story, they become one of the most profound means of revealing God to others. This is the most meaningful role a created being can have in relation to his Creator. So how did we get this so backwards? How is it that so many people are asked to invite Jesus into their lives, encouraged to envision how he might make their lives better? Could it be that well-meaning Christians, zealous to see people encounter Jesus, actually reworked God's story to make it "user friendly," and in so doing, have actually so distorted the gospel that it has become another gospel altogether (Gal. 1:6–8)?

immature
egocentric

The Story of God Is Not at Risk

God begins his story with the creation of the stage and production. Lighting is built. An environment resembling a forest preserve, including pristine water, vegetation, and animals, completes the set as God writes the first man into his story. God creates an entire ecosystem and puts man at its center. Yet man is set apart in this creation with no peer. Humans are set apart—created, yet unique from all creation by function and value. This distinction given to both male and female in Genesis 1:26–27 is called "the image of God." Being an image bearer is exactly what sets apart humanity from the rest of creation: "The human being is both a creature and a person; he or she is a created person. . . . To be a creature means that I cannot move a finger or utter a word apart from God; to be a person means that when my fingers are moved, I move them, and that when words are uttered by my lips, I utter them."[3] In order to recognize this reality about ourselves, we must first acknowledge our creatureliness in that we are utterly dependent on God and, second, take responsibility for our personhood in which we carry out physical and moral decisions every moment. The balance and combination of these two elements express how we are made in his image as created persons, which is essentially what it means to be human.

Imaging God is the most humanizing act or function a person can perform or experience. The best way to understand what it means to image God is to learn more about God and his story. As gods go, the God of the Bible reveals himself as distinct. He shows himself to be transcendent (bigger and outside of his creation) and immanent (engaged in his creation). As God engages his creation we find him sharing the governance of his creation with the humans he created (in Genesis 2:15 the man is instructed to work and keep the garden; in 2:19–20 the man names the animals God created.) We see that participating with God in his work is one way humans image God.

At this point, God declares the first "not good" of his creation, and it has to do with man being alone, so God creates a partner for the man. This gift of woman to man has many wonderful advantages. One good of this gift to Adam is that he now has another human (image bearer) with whom to image the Creator. The "not good" has a double edge to it. If the man is alone, he does not have the relational opportunity to image God to another, nor does he have the relational opportunity to experience God's being imaged from another.

As we read of Adam's response to his God-given partner (Gen. 2:23–24), we learn something significant about the image of God: it is designed to work within loving relationships. We see this later in God's story as he reveals more of his plan in the Ten Commandments. We see his commands calling for the embodiment of loving God and others. Everything God asks and expects of us is summed up in Matthew 22:37–40: "You shall love the Lord your God with all your heart and with all your soul and with all your mind. This is the great and first commandment. And a second is like it: You shall love your neighbor as yourself. On these two commandments depend all the Law and the Prophets."

This text demonstrates that God created man both to image God and to be in relationship with others (with both God and humans). There are two more clues within this first scene of God's story that inform our understanding of the image of God. They both come from observing God's interaction with the man (Gen. 2:15–17).

First, God gives the man a boundary. In a world without sin, competition, or paranoia-inducing marketing, boundaries can be good things. This boundary is an opportunity for the man to obey God, in essence, to declare God as the one he will worship through living according to God's desire or will. This helps us understand that we image God by worshiping him, and we worship him by bending our wills to his and living lives reflecting his supremacy. If something as simple as an eating habit can be a means of worship, we're compelled to take worship out of the realm of music and into venues of action, attitude, relationship— essentially all of life.

The second clue is seen in God's warning man against disobedience: "But of the tree of the knowledge of good and evil you shall not eat, for in the day that you eat of it you shall surely die" (Gen. 2:17). The penalty for disobedience is death, the destruction of or at least the radical distortion to the image bearer. Adam had no reference point for this warning; nothing on earth had died. He was left with the implication that death must be a terrible thing. We can conclude that imaging God as he intends requires life. A person who is spiritually dead, separated by sin from oneness with God, is a distorted image bearer, and though there may be ways in which God is seen, the image portrayed will be seriously impaired and distorted.

With that said, let's catapult forward to a time in God's story when there will be no death and God's transforming work will be complete. Here we find something fascinating: neither God's design nor his purpose was ever at risk. In Revelation 21 we have a re-creation scene that forms the bookend to God's story. In Revelation 21:1 God creates a new heaven and a new earth (notice God is still creator and designer). In verse 3 God dwells among his people (similar to God's walking with man in the garden). The people of God are called God's "bride" (vv. 2, 9), suggesting that we will continue to partner with God in his activity and experience a profound love relationship with him. The temple or worship center mentioned in Revelation 21 is God himself, so there can be little doubt as to our design as worshipers in the new creation. Finally, in this new creation death has died (v. 4), and we will live as image-bearing sons of God (v. 7). These bookends form an arc of unified purpose.

Chart 1.1: God's Unshakeable Design

Original Creation	New Creation
God is creator / designer	God is creator / designer
Humans are image bearers	Humans are sons of God (image bearers)
We are designed to love	We are called the bride of God
We are designed to worship	We declare the glory of God
We are designed for life	There will be no more death

Within this grand arc of the story, we learn of God's love, character, holiness, and heart to redeem people from hopeless lives of small-scale performances. *life w/o him*

Because God has invited us by design to participate with him, we see God revealing himself both through his story as told in the Bible and through the transformed lives that intersect with his story. Seeing how we reappear in his grand finale, we soon realize there are no meaningless parts in his script. *if you are a witness*

God's Story Includes Risk

If the ending is real and certain, what makes this story a story? In other words, if the outcome is secure, where's the drama? If God wins, and we're all perfected images of God living in a 1,400-cubic-mile city, why bother? The answer lies somewhere between mystery (the aspects and truths about God that are not clearly or completely revealed within his story) and authenticity (giving us roles with real experiences of love and expressions of alignment or will). As mentioned above, being human means being utterly dependent on God and yet possessing a relative ability to make significant decisions. We are real people with real choices, which is why God's story includes risk (even if the story line is not at risk). It requires faith (even when the ending is secure within his revealed framework) and shows him to be a God of grace and truth, love and holiness, power and mercy.

God's Story Is Told through His Creation

In Romans 1:20 we read, "For his invisible attributes, namely, his eternal power and divine nature, have been clearly perceived, ever since the creation of the world, in the things that have been made." Just as we learn from God's creative acts, God also leaves evidences of his existence, as though there were divine finger-prints throughout his creation for us to discover who he is and what he is like. One theologian puts it this way: "His essence, indeed, is incomprehensible, utterly transcending all human thought; but on each of his works his glory is engraved in charac-ters so bright, so distinct, and so illustrious, that none, however dull and illiterate, can plead ignorance as their excuse."[4] So it is that all of creation bears his authorship. Going a little further, if we take into account that every person bears the image of God, then we can understand every person to have some sense of God within his soul. People can visibly know the evidence of God's story in the world, and they consciously know the evidence of God's story in their own being. Having this sense of God, how-ever, is not enough to actually know his story. We have direct access to the story in physical form, the Bible.

God's Story Is Told through the Bible

Many people want to discount the Bible or debate its reliability, but the Bible does claim to be inspired by God, giving it the dis-tinct role as the record of God's story. "All Scripture is breathed out by God and profitable for teaching, for reproof, for correction, and for training in righteousness" (2 Tim. 3:16). The key reason for God's doing this supernatural work of inspiration is found in the next verse: " . . . that the man of God may be competent, equipped for every good work" (v. 17). For the purpose of this book, let's assume you are a person willing to be branded "of

God," and that you want to be competent and equipped to do good works. If this is true about you, then you are exactly the person for whom God went through the trouble of inspiring and preserving his Word. At this point, we can agree that God's Word is sufficient for us to know the story of God.[5] God has done far more than give us a story of revelation; he has revealed himself to us for our transformation.

God's Story Is Told through Jesus

The über-disclosure of God is in Jesus Christ, the God-man, and the next chapter is dedicated to his heroic role in the story. Many have argued that Jesus was just another ordinary man who made some waves during the first century AD. Hebrews 1:3 makes a noteworthy claim to the contrary: "He is the radiance of the glory of God and the exact imprint of his nature, and he upholds the universe by the word of his power." Viewing Jesus's life in particular is most beneficial for knowing God and his story. Also, Hebrews 2:4 tells us God bore witness to Jesus through signs and wonders displayed in Jesus's life and ministry. It's surprising, though, to realize that many of the miracles Jesus performed were also performed by other men. Jesus raises people from the dead (Luke 7:11–17; John 11:33–44) as do Elijah (1 Kings 17) and Paul (Acts 20:8–12). Jesus walks on water, as does Peter ever so briefly (Matt. 14:28–31). Jesus heals the lame (John 5:1–9), and Peter does, too (Acts 3:1–8). Jesus exorcises demons (Matt. 9:32–34) as do those he has commissioned (Luke 10:17). So what difference does it make that Jesus performed all of these miracles?

What Hebrews is telling us is similar to why God gave Moses the two signs of a staff turning into a serpent and a hand with an on/off switch for leprosy (Ex. 4:1–8). God gave those signs to Moses so people would believe that he was saying something from God. Jesus's miracles, for the most part, were God's flashing neon sign saying "truth told here." So, his miracles were not so much to prove his deity as to prove his authenticity. When he said things such as, "Before Abraham was, I am" and "I am the bread [true manna] of life" and "Your sins are forgiven," he was speaking New Testament culture's cues for "I am God." Isn't it ironic that the God whom the religious leaders believed Jesus was blaspheming was in fact providing signs and wonders as a means of saying about Jesus, "He's not blaspheming; he's telling the truth"?

The Story of God Is Told through the Trinity

God makes himself known in his story as a triune God.[6] Here are just a couple of examples from the Old Testament that hint at a multi-person deity. First, in Genesis 1, our first scene, there was a holy deliberation over the creation of man: "Then God said, 'Let us make man in our image, after our likeness'" (v. 26). While many debate the legitimacy of understanding God as speaking to other persons of the Godhead in this verse, other options are not more convincing and seem to come from a zeal to disprove the Trinity rather than to interpret this text in light of the whole of Scripture.

Second, strange as it may sound at first, the other example comes from a verse that seems to disprove the Trinity. "Hear, O Israel: The LORD our God, the LORD is one" (Deut. 6:4). This statement sounds like there is no room for three, yet this same word, *echad*, is used for "one" in Genesis 2:24, showing "one" as a composite of two persons as one flesh.[7] This oneness of God in Deuteronomy simply informs us that there are not three separate deities. Our theological model of Trinity must therefore understand God as one God composed of three persons. The metaphor of oneness in marriage is used in many places within God's story to help us understand oneness, belonging, identity, and equality, both within the Godhead and in our relationships.

Picture the Trinity, this divine community, at work in creation. "In the beginning, God [the Father] created the heavens and the earth" (Gen. 1:1). Throughout Genesis 1, God says or speaks (the word of God) everything into existence. Jesus is called "the Word" of God in John 1:1–5. And in Genesis 1:2 we read that the Spirit of God was hovering over the waters of the earth. All three persons of the Godhead were working to bring about the creation of the universe. Now consider the objections of your friends or maybe even objections you have raised because it all seems like an egocentric God created people just to worship him. What a different picture it is if the Father longs to have people worship his Son and the Spirit, the Son longs for people to worship the Father and the Spirit, and the Spirit longs for image bearers to worship the Father and the Son.

A creative, eternal community loving one another and exalting God is fertile soil for harvesting insights in what it means to image God. The doctrine of the Trinity becomes crucial to our understanding of biblical community and how it serves as the environment for each of us to image our God one to another. Bruce Ware sums it up:

> We should look not only to the character of God, and to the commands of God, but also to the triune roles and relationships among the Triune Persons of God to see what it means to live our lives as his images. We are created to reflect what God is like, and this includes a reflection of the personal relationships within the Trinity.[8]

The more we observe the Trinity's communication, roles, and esteem for one another, the more we will understand that equality or value is not defined by a role or function. Some would rather reject the doctrine of the Trinity, or at least alter it by cutting all ties with hierarchy, submission, or submissive roles rather than learn from this Trinitarian God what imaging God's glory looks like.

The New Testament develops our understanding of the Trinity, their interaction as loving and mutually esteeming, and their exceeding comfort with roles that obey, defer, or give preeminence to one another. Philippians 2 is a passage of theological land mines, while at the same a time a gold mine for providing a beautiful portrayal of the image of God. In Philippians 2:5, we are encouraged to "have this mind among yourselves, which is yours in Christ Jesus." Paul definitely tells us Jesus is a template for our thinking. He then goes on to describe Jesus leaving his awesome position in heaven and coming to earth as human, as servant, and as obedient unto death. This so pleases the Father (which was Jesus's motive) that the Father exalts Jesus to the highest position the universe affords (Phil. 2:9–11).

If we stop with seeing what the Father does to the Son, we miss the relational interplay of a loving community of peers in the last part of verse 11. Jesus uses his high position to glorify God the Father. Here is a picture of this holy, divine community esteeming one another. Jesus embraces death to please the Father, the Father decorates his Son the war hero with the kingdom, and the Son then uses his kingdom to exalt the Father. The Father is definitely seen as the one able to give the highest position, yet the Son uses both his lowest position and his highest position to please and honor the Father.

Now consider this short list of activities and truths about the Holy Spirit:

- He points to Christ (John 15:26).
- He makes known the things of God (1 Cor. 2:9–12).
- He intercedes for us (Rom. 8:26) as does Jesus (1 John 2:1).
- He has been sent by the Father and the Son (John 13:16–17; 16:7).
- The Holy Spirit's presence and work correspond to having Jesus with us in the flesh (in John 14:16 Jesus calls the Spirit "another Helper").

In John 14:16, do you see that Jesus wasn't saying that there would be a force or a redeeming memory of himself? This situation is not the same as when a loved one passes on and mourners are comforted by thinking, "I'll always have him with me in my heart." The Holy Spirit is a very real person commissioned from the chamber of heaven. The Holy Spirit is as much sent to earth to work in the hearts of men as was Jesus.

The God telling the story has made it mysteriously clear. He is one, yet he is three persons. These three persons are all integrally involved in the story as God, yet they assume complementary roles. These roles are not a show of force as to which God will submit to the other. No, these persons are involved in revealing the other persons of the Godhead through reflection or imaging through relationship and interaction. As image bearers in the story of God, we do well to learn from their example.[9]

The Story of God Involves Conflict

God has written his story within the context of a cosmic battle. God established his rule beyond this earthly scene, and the first acts of rebellion took place offstage. We are given small clues of what went down. Isaiah 14:13–14 depicts what was going on within the heart of Satan: "You said in your heart, 'I will ascend to heaven; above the stars of God I will set my throne on high; I will sit on the mount of assembly in the far reaches of the north; I will ascend above the heights of the clouds; I will make myself like the Most High.'" Satan's sin is that of pride and trying to take the place of God on his throne.[10] Then, Ezekiel 28:13–17 gives some further detail as to the original created state of the beautiful angel God created, and how he distorted God's design:

> You were in Eden, the garden of God;
> > every precious stone was your covering....
> On the day that you were created
> > they were prepared.
> You were an anointed guardian cherub.
> > I placed you; you were on the holy mountain of God;
> > in the midst of the stones of fire you walked.

You were blameless in your ways
    from the day you were created,
    till unrighteousness was found in you.
In the abundance of your trade
    you were filled with violence in your midst, and you sinned;
so I cast you as a profane thing from the mountain of God,
    and I destroyed you, O guardian cherub,
    from the midst of the stones of fire.
Your heart was proud because of your beauty;
    you corrupted your wisdom for the sake of your splendor.
I cast you to the ground;
    I exposed you before kings,
    to feast their eyes on you.[11]

Ezekiel 28:17 is profoundly offensive; it depicts a created being using his assets or ability for his own sake or splendor, robbing the glory due his Creator. We have just seen how the Godhead rolls. The Father gives the Son center stage, the Son uses his limelight to glorify the Father, and the Spirit reveals the things of God to men and glorifies Jesus. The paradigm for created beings is the Creator in tri-unity of persons. They exalt one another, and we have been created to do the same—to bring glory to our Creator. Satan became a glory grabber and set in motion an entire battle of rebellion to overthrow a kingdom whose rule and subjects glorify God.

As we begin reading the story in Genesis, we don't know that this insurrection happened. A materialistic or scientific mind, conditioned to believe only what can be "objectively verified," is certainly thrown into a death-gripping spiral dive when Genesis 3 is read. Almost out of nowhere, our eyes fall on "serpent." The Serpent talks to Eve. Reasoning her out of her convictions and convincing her that God himself had malevolent purposes for establishing her boundaries, this Serpent seems to have had some ability to assert his agenda onto the situation. The Serpent was able to distort the boundaries God had established for Adam and Eve. He turned obedience into constriction rather than opportunity and worshiping God and declaring him worthy of loving obedience to rules about power and self. Perhaps the most appealing thing about this temptation to Eve and Adam was not the promise of knowing good and evil but actually having the authority to name good and evil. In God's story, God alone declares what is good and what is evil. In a rebel state where personal wisdom is brokered for the sake of one's own splendor (Ezek. 28:17), temptation looms large to have one's own throne and to make oneself the highest court of appeals (Isa. 14:13–14).

It is clear from how the story is crafted that Satan generates evil, though he was created good and for good. Take notice of two huge implications from the story: first, Satan is created, and evil is therefore not an eternal counterbalance to good; and, second, because evil is written in as part of the story, it can be ultimately written out. Humans, while created good, were lured into an evil choice, and from that fateful moment their image bearing has been distorted by sin, and they have been generators of sin. Since that moment, man has struggled against imaging someone or something other than his Creator.

God's Story Involves Rescue

Sin's impact was completely devastating to God's original creation. The imaging we were intended to do is no longer possible. We were designed to magnify God (Isa. 43:7; 1 Cor. 10:31; Eph. 1:11–12). Think for a moment of a telescope as a magnifying instrument. It is unique in how it magnifies. While a microscope magnifies a smaller object to make it appear bigger, the telescope magnifies an object (such as a star or a planet) so that it appears clearer than can be observed by the eye. Yet the object is actually bigger than the image seen through the telescope.[12] God uses the experience of others to let us observe him in action, yet he is much bigger than the actions we observe. So, as image bearers, we have the capacity to magnify the object that we worship. When that object is people, stuff, problems, or fears, we become idolaters, and when we magnify our Creator, we are worshipers.

This past year I stood at a Communion table to pray with people about fears that were keeping them from drawing near to God. The list included:

- The fear of failing.
- The fear of rejection.
- The fear of abandonment.

I listed these by how frequently they were mentioned, but now let's fill out the list by adding "another person":

- The fear of failing *another person*.
- The fear of being rejected by *another person*.
- The fear of abandonment by *another person*.

See how simple and subtle it is to use our ability to magnify and put someone else in the spot that belongs to God? It is the act of making an idol. "[An idol] is anything more important to you than God, anything that absorbs your heart and imagination more than God, anything you seek to give you what only God can give."[13] In the cases above, idolatry devolved from something each person thought would be fulfilling to something fearful. The truth is that an idol cannot perform as God's peer, yet we try to suppress this truth, afraid we will never be rescued (Rom. 1:18). Add to this dread of no rescue by our idols the terror stemming from the self-awareness of our inability or failed attempts to rescue ourselves, and we have a front-row seat for observing the paralyzed soul of a marred image bearer. One person at our Communion experience expressed fears concerning God himself. She wrote her fear honestly: "I am afraid that God isn't big enough to redeem me from my sin."

We seldom think that the stars we see in our darkened sky are balls of fire bigger than the sun, and we seldom think the God we see, distorted by sinfulness, can possibly be bigger than our sin or fear.[14] The story of God requires redemption, God-sized redemption. Something that could be simply remedied with more good than bad in my behavior can't even cover the downside of a story my size, let alone a story of global and historical proportions. Without a big story and a bigger God, we are left trying to rescript our personal meaning, as did Satan himself. We really are childish in our scripting ability, preferring overt experiences of gratification rather than artistically crafted good works prepared for us through Christ (Eph. 2:10).

The good news to the cosmic battle and redemptive story of God is that the victory is already in view in Revelation 21. These redemptive elements to the story are not only ultimate but personal. God scripts the times and the events of his story so that our part may be a venue for imaging God. In fact, we see cycles of redemption in the history of Israel as well as in the history of the church. We also see patterns of transformation within the people of God's story. These patterns then become the benchmarks of God's work in a person's life. God is a great author, and he brings unique caveats to each scene, yet he draws some recurring qualities together in the biographies of his people. These qualities are similar because it is the same God who is transforming each cast member, conforming all to the image of sonship as embodied in the life of Jesus.

There are four arenas common to everyone who experiences God's redemptive grace within his story.

1) Redeemed to Reflect God's Image

The first arena is that of *his redemptive work of rescuing us from our sin, transforming us into image bearers, giving us a rightful identity as a child of God, and restoring our capacity to trust, love, worship, and please him.* "Redemption is God's act of releasing his people from an alien power, and of bringing them to freedom so that they can live as his people according to the covenant promises."[15] The most shocking aspect to his story is that humans are redeemable beings. Angels were faced with aligning themselves with God or with his adversary Satan, but there was no rebounding, no help or helper given to them to bring them from anarchists to ones accepted. Peter tells us that the angels watch closely this redemptive story of God's (1 Pet. 1:12). They do not get to experience redemption, and so they must watch and see how we are rescued from those who image false gods and are made into refined image bearers of God's design.

2) Reflecting God's Glory to Him through Worship

A second arena closely related to God's redemption of his people is *their ability to respond correctly to him—our worship*. God invites us into his story to bring him glory. The best way I can bring God glory is to live my life as one who worships our triune God in spirit and in truth (John 4:23–24). He recalibrates everything about me: my thoughts, my actions, and my relationships in such a way that they can all be turned back toward him as worship, just as we read in Philippians 2 of how Jesus did. While I must battle the Serpent and resist temptations to live my life for my own splendor or glory, the Holy Spirit dwells within me and empowers me to image God accurately. Paul tells us that our bodies are temples of the Holy Spirit (1 Cor. 6:19) and instruments of worship (Rom. 12:1).

One of my fantasies is being a world-class musician. I would love to be an accomplished instrumentalist. The Scriptures nearly describe our bodies in terms of worship instruments, which means I can tune my life to the key of God and live as a world-class instrumentalist, using my body to declare the praises and glory of God. Are you starting to see the significance God has scripted for your role in his story? It is life giving to think God reconciled us to himself so that we can worship him while at the same time demolish the idols that ruin us.

3) Reflecting God's Glory to One Another through Community

A third arena is the new belonging available as *members of the rescued people of God*. Not only does Paul describe our personal bodies as a temple of the Holy Spirit, but he describes gospel communities as temples of God: "Do you not know that you are God's temple and that God's Spirit dwells in you? If anyone destroys God's temple, God will destroy him. For God's temple is holy, and you are that temple" (1 Cor. 3:16–17). There Paul uses a plural "you" to describe God's temple, suggesting he is talking about the church at Corinth. The New Testament is full of wonderful descriptions of who we are as a people of God. Community is the way God's story and redemptive work is best experienced. Dietrich Bonhoeffer states that "the goal of all Christian community [is that] they meet one another as bringers of the message of salvation."[16] There are few commands in Scripture that do not have social implications; the plurality of salvation is too often overlooked in the Western church, and perhaps it is one of the greatest reasons we do not often experience salvation as described in the New Testament.

4) The Mission of Reflecting God's Glory in a Fallen World

The fourth arena impacts the *people with whom we share the planet*, but not the hope that is found in Jesus as the hero of God's story. With regard to the story of God, we are going to call this "mission," taking the kingdom of God to edges of faithlessness and living an edgy, incarnational faith. When we define *faithed* and *non-faithed* people groups in ways that give permission to disconnect from neighbors, it is a harmful distinction. When God's story calls us to love and image God as a redemptive presence with responses calling for an explanation from lives fueled by hope (1 Pet. 3:15), we see the value of getting caught following Jesus. God's story compels us to join him on mission. This mission includes relating to unbelieving neighbors, family, and friends closely enough so that they can observe us imaging God before their very eyes. It also includes joining forces with other believers to bring community within the context of daily living. "Most gospel ministry involves ordinary people doing ordinary things with gospel intentionality."[17] God delights in sharing his mission with us, and our participating with God in his activity is what it means to image God.

Conclusion

Let's end this chapter by regrouping around the story of God. God has a design for a kingdom in which Jesus is king. Each member of the Trinity glorifies the others and desires a kingdom full of people who do the same by authentically imaging God with their lives, not merely with their behavior. This kingdom was launched in the garden but was short-lived when the prehistoric rebel came into history as a serpent, leading Adam and Eve into rebellion by defying God's rule and reign. Humans, as bearers of the image of God, were ruined by this act of sin, and the distortion of the design extends throughout God's creation.

God's story recycles through nations and epics as well as through the lives of individuals. Our great hope is that God has declared humans redeemable. God didn't come to earth as a nation, as a culture, or even as a church, but he came as Jesus Christ, the Son of God. This means nations and empires may come and go, cultures may transition, and churches may start and close, but God's story is not at risk, and his children will not fade away into annihilation. The people of God are an eternal people, and the redeeming work of God is an eternal work, so, as a person and as a people of God, we can have hope in the God of the story.

Revelation 2 and 3 serve as a great example of identity drift. Five out of the seven churches Jesus addresses are told to repent or be disciplined. God tells these people he cannot be blackmailed into blessing a particular expression of his church just because it is called "church." The church as the bride of Christ is found in Revelation 21, but the church found on 15th and Anywhere Streets does not have the same hope. Our greatest hope as a church is to be a community of God's people on mission, bringing him glory as image bearers.

In the Sistine Chapel, Michelangelo painted 12,000 square feet of the chapel ceiling between 1508 and 1512, containing over three hundred biblical characters. Michelangelo was originally approached about painting the chapel ceiling with a view toward creating frescoes around the twelve apostles. He turned down the offer and was eventually given freedom to include the characters of his choosing. Somehow, Michelangelo felt that even the apostles, without the context of God's redemptive story, did not warrant the time and effort it would take him to paint this ceiling. When given the freedom to portray God's majestic story, he could not do a series of fly-by paintings; he had to include God's story as he understood it.

In Michelangelo's depiction of God's story, Jesus figures predominately in the final judgment. For Michelangelo, the story is not epic without the creation being completely restored and redeemed from the rebel assault mounted on it and against God. This painted ceiling is thought by many to be Michelangelo's greatest work. What makes it amazing is its vastness. Had it been a mere collection of smaller works tastefully framed, it would not be the same as this stunning retelling of God's kingdom story. Lives, as amazing as they are, can never be a crowning achievement when lived within their own frame. To be part of something so sweeping as the story of God elevates an ordinary day, event, or life to being part of the greatest work on earth. It makes us someone with the ability to image the wonder of our artistic Creator, and to do it in a way that points hearts to their greatest longing—personal connection to the only one who can name us meaningful.

CHAPTER 1 ASSIGNMENT

After each chapter there will be sets of assignments. The first set is designed to help you encounter some of the biblical truths discussed within the chapter. The second set is designed to help establish convictions and dislodge distortions by explaining more of what the Bible has to say on following Jesus.

Exposure to God and His Story
Creation (John 1:1–3)
Redemption (John 3:16–17; 20:21–23)
Trinity (John 3:17; 14:26; 17:3)
Revelation (1 Tim. 3:16–17)
Passion (Matt. 28:18–20)

Digging Deeper
Below are twenty-seven references on the Trinity.[18] Take time to journal and pray through them.

1) Covenant promise (Lev. 26:12; Rev. 21:3).
2) The Father gave a people to the Son (John 6:37; 17:6).
3) Father and Son send the Spirit to indwell believers (John 14:23).
4) God becomes our God and Father through Jesus (Matt. 6:9; John 20:17; 2 Cor. 6:16–18).
5) We share in overflow of the Father's eternal love for the Son and the Spirit (John 1:12).
6) We are grafted as branches into the true vine, God's Son (John 15:1–11; 17:26).
7) We experience our union with the Son enabled by the Spirit (John 1:12–13; 6:44–45; 15:3).
8) Our union with Jesus grows (John 8:31–32; 15:4–11).
9) Our task is carrying on the apostolic mission (John 17:18; 20:21–22).
10) The goal is to glorify the Father in the Son (John 14:13).
11) The Holy Spirit rests and remains in our midst (John 14:17).

12) The Holy Spirit guides into the way, the truth, and the life (John 14:6; 6:63; 16:13–15).

13) The Spirit's work complements Jesus's earthly mission (John 14:17–18).

14) The Spirit's presence completes God's Trinitarian dwelling with his people (John 14:1–3, 16).

Our Salvation through the Trinity

15) God gives life to those who believe (John 3:16; 17:2–3; 20:31).

16) Personal knowledge of God the Father through God the Son (John 17:3).

17) Knowledge enabled by God the Holy Spirit (John 15:26; 16:13–15).

18) Confirmed fellowship with Father and Son by the giving of the Spirit (1 John 1:3; 4:13).

The Glory of the Trinity

19) The Father reveals his name through the Son (John 12:28).

20) The Father's self-disclosure through Jesus, ultimately on the cross (John 10:15, 17–18).

21) Jesus's exaltation and glorification (John 7:39; 12:23; 17:1).

22) The Father and the Son mutually glorify one another (John 13:32).

23) The Son gives of the Father's rich blessing by declaring it to future believers (John 16:14).

The Trinity on Mission

24) The Son is sent by the Father and sends the Spirit (John 15:26; 16:7).

25) Jesus prays for himself (John 17:1–5).

26) Jesus prays for disciples (John 17:6–19).

27) Jesus prays for future believers (John 17:20–26).

2

THE HERO OF THE STORY

I have some hopeless movie-watching friends. I don't mean they watch too many movies but that they are really bad at watching movies. They can't keep characters, relationships, or plotlines straight. When we watch a movie together, I dread them leaving the room, because when they return, it is a massive undertaking to get them caught up on what they've missed. I sometimes go through a similar thing when trying to tell someone about Jesus when he doesn't know anything of the story of God. For instance, I'll say, "Well, he is the one God was talking about who was the seed of the woman who would bruise the head of the Serpent (Gen. 3:15), and he is the offspring promised to Abraham who will bless the rest of the earth (Gal. 3:16)," or, "He is the one who will reign on David's throne forever (2 Sam. 7:12–13). Does that make sense?"

Jesus Is God and Man

It can be very disturbing when people inject out-of-context pictures of Jesus into everyday life and let people draw their own conclusions about who he is. The misconceptions that result allow people to take principles from Jesus's life and run companies; build political organizations; buy or not buy houses; educate their children at home, in Christian school, or in public school; and do it all dogmatically in the name of Jesus. Without a context (the story of God) for Jesus, he can become the proof-text for whatever anyone wants to do.[1] At that point, he is no longer the hero of

God's story, but the one making a cameo appearance in someone else's story. To see Jesus in the story of God means that we look at everything God has done, including every person God has put into his script, and we discover *how all image God like Jesus did.*

The opening line of Scripture introduces us to its hero, God. Throughout the pages of Scripture this God is revealed. In the closing line of the New Testament Scriptures, we are reminded that the God who is the hero of the true story of Scripture is Jesus Christ. . . .

Following his resurrection, Jesus opened the Old Testament to teach others about himself: "Beginning with Moses and all the Prophets, he interpreted to them in all the Scriptures the things concerning himself" (Luke 24:27). Likewise, in speaking to his disciples, Jesus said, "These are my words that I spoke to you while I was still with you, that everything written about me in the Law of Moses and the Prophets and the Psalms must be fulfilled" (Luke 24:44). . . .

Unlike the first Adam, Jesus Christ is the Last Adam who passed his test in a garden and in so doing imputed his righteousness to us to overcome the sin imputed to us through the sin of the first Adam. Jesus is the true and better Abel who, although he was innocent, was slain and whose blood cries out for our acquittal. When Abraham left his father and home, he was doing the same thing that Jesus would do when he left heaven. When Isaac carried his own wood and laid down his life to be sacrificed at the hand of his father Abraham, he was showing us what Jesus would later do. Jesus is the greater Jacob, who wrestled with God in Gethsemane and, though wounded and limping, walked away from his grave blessed. Jesus is the greater Joseph who serves at the right hand of God the King, extends forgiveness and provision to those of us who have betrayed him, and uses his power to save us in loving reconciliation. Jesus is greater than Moses in that he stands as a mediator between God and us, bringing us the New Covenant. Like Job, innocent Jesus suffered and was tormented by the Devil so that God might be glorified, while his dumb friends were no help or encouragement. Jesus is a King greater than David, who has slain our giants of Satan, sin, and death, although in the eyes of the world he was certain to face a crushing defeat at their hands. Jesus is greater than Jonah in that he spent three days in the grave and not just a fish to save a multitude even greater than Nineveh.

Furthermore, when Boaz redeemed Ruth and brought her and her despised people into community with God's people, he was showing what Jesus would do to redeem his bride the church from all the nations of the earth. When Nehemiah rebuilt Jerusalem, he was doing something similar to Jesus, who is building for us a New Jerusalem as our eternal home. When Hosea married an unfaithful whoring wife whom he continued to pursue in love, he was showing us the heart of Jesus, who does the same for his unfaithful bride, the church. Finally, when God's people sought to keep their homes free from filth through various Old Testament rituals, they were showing that their lives were filled with the filth of sin and they desperately needed Jesus to come and make them clean.[2]

In writing his Gospel, John seems to take a different approach and plunges people right in to who Jesus is and what he was doing here on earth:

> In the beginning was the Word, and the Word was with God, and the Word was God. He was in the beginning with God. All things were made through him, and without him was not any thing made that was made. In him was life, and the life was the light of men. The light shines in the darkness, and the darkness has not overcome it. (John 1:1–5)

As we journey through Scripture, we are often struck with questions such as, "What does *that* mean?" or, "What the heck is God saying here?" Here are some quick "what the hecks" that jump off the page to me:

- The beginning of *what*?
- How is the *Word* already at the beginning?
- How can the Word be *with God* and *be God*?

John, however, knows his audience and the framework it brings, and he has left enough clues for his readers to enter the story of God as the context for his Gospel. John assumes his readers can embrace the thought of God being more than one person yet not being more than one God. John assumes his readers know what the beginning is, which most likely is creation, since all things were made through him, and that in him was life (vv. 3–4). This requires the Word to be a noncreated, preexistent, living creator—that sounds a lot like God. John tells us that Jesus (described as "the Word," John 1:1) has existed eternally "with God" as "God." John further describes this Word as the agent of God's creative work (John 1:3–5), the one in whom divine life resides and through whom God's creative light shines forth in the darkness (cf. Gen. 1:3).[3] Those of us on the post-resurrection side of the historical continuum are at a very privileged position, able to see Scripture and the story of God. Imagine if we were in the unfolding drama of the Old Testament, we would see our hope and understanding of God and his kingdom dwindling with man's every turning point.

Chart 2.1: Shrinking Hope

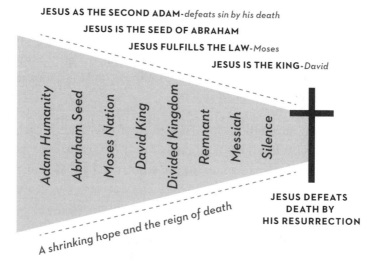

But when we have eyes to see that Jesus is the hero of the story, we get a more full-orbed picture of his plan. His coming is promised in the midst of the curse; he is the seed of Abraham; he is the king who will reign on David's throne; he is the Messiah; and his life, death, and resurrection inaugurated in hope giving form to the kingdom of God.

Chart 2.2: Increasing Hope

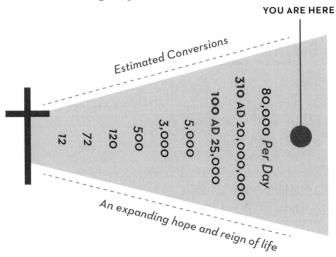

Jesus Receives His Identity from the Father

Jesus walks onto the scene during a time of shrunken hope. He walks in, however, knowing he is *the hope*—the Christ, the Messiah of God. Yet his hope is not in what he is going to do as much as it is in his God, his Father. Jesus interacts relationally with the Father in ways completely foreign to mere religion. In fact, the very idea that he would call God his Father smacked of blasphemy to the religious (John 5:18). Nevertheless, from a young age Jesus saw God as his personal Father (Luke 2:49), not merely as an impersonal parental figure to a generic, collective Israel. Later, at Jesus's baptism, the Father manifests himself in a voice saying, "This is my beloved Son, with whom I am well pleased" (Matt. 3:17). From a horizontal or human perspective this encounter is huge because Jesus hadn't yet performed any miracles, cast out any demons, taught a parable, or given a single sermon.

The wow factor of signs and wonders, which drew crowds (John 6:2), was not in gear, and still Jesus is told by his heavenly Father that he is loved and pleasing to him. Can you pause here long enough to sense what it would be like to hear a voice from heaven tell you, "I love you," or, "You give me great pleasure"? Don't discount it or sidestep it with your mental disclaimers of why it could never happen, or why God would never say that about you. Accept it; being loved is part of being a child of God:

> See what kind of love the Father has given to us, that we should be called children of God. (1 John 3:1)
>
> In this is love, not that we have loved God but that he loved us. (1 John 4:10)
>
> In love he predestined us for adoption as sons through Jesus Christ, according to the purpose of his will, to the praise of his glorious grace, with which he has blessed us in the Beloved. (Eph. 1:4–6)
>
> But to all who did receive him, who believed in his name, he gave the right to become children of God, who were born, not of blood nor of the will of the flesh nor of the will of man, but of God. (John 1:12–13)

These verses tell us we are loved as God's children, loved before we ever loved God, chosen in love for his purposes and pleasure. God takes such delight because it results in "one great ultimate purpose—that the glory of his grace might be praised forever and ever with white-hot affection."[4]

Take a few minutes and read John 17. Listen for how Jesus interacts with his Father during the final hours of his life. Jesus speaks the name "Father" six times in this prayer, and the entire prayer is addressed to the Father. In the Sermon on the Mount (Matthew 5–7), Jesus instructs about prayer and speaks of praying to the Father: "Pray to your Father" (6:6), and "Your Father knows what you need before you ask him" (6:8). He then gives a paradigm for praying and begins his model prayer with "Our Father."

Jesus is quite aware of the Father's personal presence and direction in his own life (John 5:19). From Jesus's life we see a model of what it looks like to be God-centered. Jesus doesn't pull out his platinum God card, borrowing power or strength to cope his way through his temptations sinlessly; he lives within the limited equity of a human life bound by dependence upon God as his loving Father.

The Holy Spirit joins the Father and Son at Jesus's baptism, appearing as a dove (Matt. 3:16). He then leads Jesus (Matt. 4:1) into the wilderness where he is tempted by the Devil. Hebrews 4:15 tells us that Jesus was tempted in every respect as we are tempted, yet he did not sin. This is a testimony of Jesus's loving obedience to the Father through the working of the Holy Spirit in his life. We see the Spirit manifesting an aspect of his fruit (Gal. 5:22–23) in Luke 10:21, where Jesus is described as being filled with joy or rejoicing in the Holy Spirit with thanks to the Father for revealing truths to those who had joined him on his mission. Here is Jesus, Son of God, living a dependent life; he seeks direction and identity from the Father and the Spirit and sees himself as partnering with the Father in his work (John 17:4). Anthony Hoekema explains:

> As a skillful teacher uses visual aids to help his or her pupils understand what is being taught, so God the Father has given us in Jesus Christ a visual example of what the image of God is. There is no better way of seeing the image of God than to look at Jesus Christ. What we see and hear in Christ is what God intended for man . . . [and] if it is true that Christ perfectly images God, then the heart of the image of God must be love. For no man ever loved as Christ loved.[5]

Jesus's life illustrates for us that, by the Spirit's indwelling, humans are empowered to love God and others with the same love existing within the intra-Trinitarian relationship and with God's love for the whole world. Jesus models for us what it looks like to get our identity from God by living out our role in his story.

Jesus Expresses His Identity as a Worshiper

As we have observed, Jesus's life was one of prayer. John 17 shows us many things about Jesus's perspective and priorities. Listen to his prayer and see how he assesses his earthly ministry:

- "I glorified you on earth, having accomplished the work that you gave me to do." (v. 4)
- "I have manifested your name to the people whom you gave me out of the world." (v. 6)
- "I have given them the words that you gave me." (v. 8)
- "I made known to them your name." (v. 26)

Jesus believed he was sent to glorify the Father, and glorifying the Father for Jesus meant imaging him in such a way that his name was manifested, his word was shared, his name was known, and his work was done.

This is a big picture of what it means to worship God. Worship is so much more than music. When Jesus spoke truth, he was worshiping, and when Jesus imaged the Father with his behavior, he was worshiping. When Jesus took on the nature of a human, he took on the responsibility to do the work of worship. With every breath, every thought, every action, and every relationship, he had the opportunity to image God, and he took it. He lived a sacramental life, finding a way to declare his role in the story as *sacred*. He lived life without regret. He lived his life to the full. In fact, he described this full or abundant life as what he came to offer others as well: "I came that they may have life and have it abundantly" (John 10:10).

Describing worshipful living in purely behavioral objectives gives it the stench of self-help. Sacramental or worshipful living is the fine art of combining heart with expression. If there is no heart, we have religion that yields a proud and religious spirit or cynicism that judges others and justifies self. If there is no expression, action, or behavior, then we are left with an abstract philosophical theory devoid of transformation. Neither of these is what Jesus modeled or died to provide.

Worship Comes from a Loving Heart

Scripture is clear: worship comes from a heart of love (Matt. 22:34–40). Why does someone love God? Satan told God that the main reason Job worshiped and loved God was that God blessed him (Job 1:9–10). Satan went on to suggest that if Job's blessings were lost, he would no longer worship God (1:11). God granted permission for the hedge of protection to be removed from Job, and tragedy struck. Reports came in as quickly as if they were being tweeted: enemy marauders, fire falling from heaven, severe winds. At the end of the day Job lost all his assets and all ten of his children.

In light of this, Job 1:20 is all the more profound. Upon hearing all this bad news Job tore his clothes, shaved his head, and fell to the ground in worship. That last phrase comes as a complete surprise to those who think of worship as an ecstatic experience. Job was 180 degrees removed from ecstatic, but he was not removed from a worshipful posture that gave God supremacy and declared God greater than his blessings. This intimate picture of Job's response shows us a man striving to find God in the circumstances of his life, even the painful, sorrowful ones.

It is our capacity to declare God as our stimulus that marks us as image-bearing creatures rather than as Pavlovian dogs who must respond by instinct or conditioned response. When we realign our hearts to loving God above his blessings, and when we reverence him as the only one entitled to be praised or pleased, we will find the freedom to worship without the conditioned response of circumstances.

We are prone to worship one of our greatest idols—a sense of entitlement. It is curious that Jesus did not function with a sense of entitlement, yet he fiercely guarded God the Father's right or entitlement to be worshiped above all else. Take note of these examples:

- Jesus challenged religious hypocrisy, warning against doing religious acts for recognition (Matt. 6:1, 4–6, 16–18).
- Jesus opposed religious scam artists (Matt. 23:23).
- Jesus exposed unbelief (Matt. 23:27–28; John 18:33–35).
- Jesus silenced demons because they identified him with contempt, not worship (Mark 1:34).
- Jesus honored the historical works of God without over-legitimizing the traditions of man (Matt. 12:1–8).

Jesus Worshiped in Obedience to the Father

Jesus's behavior was tightly tied to his understanding of the Father. In fact, Jesus told the religious leaders that their lifestyle reflected that they did not know the Father, nor did these leaders recognize love for the Father when it was worshipfully lived out before their very eyes (John 5:37–44). Many of the religious leaders of Jesus's day were under the impression that Rome was simply the rod of discipline God was using with his children, Israel. They thought that if they could just get Israel to adhere more closely to the law of God, God would relent from his discipline and restore them as a nation. Jesus posed a horrifying threat to their type of thinking when he called for internal renewal rather than for behavior modification (Mark 3:1–6). While Jesus adhered to the law of God, he violated current religious mores (Matt. 15:1–6). Jesus saw the religious climate of his day as spiritual abuse (Matt. 23:4).

In attempts to avoid legalism or mere conformity, often an appeal is made to freedom. Freedom, however, is usually defined as "I can do whatever I want." The argument then continues: "If

I am not free to do what I want, I am not free." This argument, however, is philosophically flawed and biblically inaccurate.[6]

I hope the following story from my family's beach holiday illustrates a different way of understanding freedom. Several years ago my family went on vacation to the Oregon coast. We bought a kite that depicted the *Peanuts* character Snoopy and over five hundred feet of string. We attached the string and launched kite Snoopy. He shot up several hundred feet into the air and hovered over the ocean. While we were enjoying our achievement, we could hear a distant noise that sounded like a repeating thump or thud. As the noise got closer we realized it was a helicopter. We tried frantically to reel in kite Snoopy, but he was too far out. The helicopter buzzed through the kite string like a hot knife through butter. As we sadly watched the sky, we saw Snoopy, still far in the air, wafting downward toward the ocean waves. I remember thinking that if I were that kite, I would have relished the sense of freedom. But the freedom was short-lived; the kite soon hit the water and was destroyed. It is ironic that the kite was actually most free when tethered by the string to the one flying it. Cut off from the string, it could not do what it was designed to do.

Similarly, we are not free when we are on our own, untethered from the one who created us and unable to do what he designed us to do. So-called religious behavior can give a false sense of security because it makes us feel like we are tethered to God, even though it does not guarantee that we are. If we are not truly tethered, we will waft our way to certain destruction.

Jesus lived the wonderful balance of catching the wind of the Holy Spirit and enjoying the gusts and swirls of life while tethered to the person and character of his Father. Jesus obeyed where Adam (1 Cor. 15:21–22), Israel (Ezek. 20:12–13), and every person on earth has not obeyed (Rom. 3:10–12). The Father is exalted by our obedience, which means our obedience is an expression of worship. When our God is seen through our obedience to him, we are functioning as image bearers, and life is lived according to the design Jesus called abundant and free (John 10:10).

It is amazing enough that Jesus lived a perfect life, but even more amazing that he did so in the midst of a fallen world and sinful people:

- His mother and father did not understand him (Luke 2:49–50).
- His brothers mocked his mission (John 7:3–5).
- His hometown didn't believe him (Matt. 13:54–58).
- His disciples stumbled over their own agendas and ambition (Mark 9:33–34).

That Jesus lived authentically amidst such an environment reveals that community was a nonnegotiable for him. John tells us that at the beginning of Jesus's ministry, many believed in Jesus's name because of the signs he performed, yet he did not entrust himself to them (John 2:24). At the end of Jesus's ministry, Luke tells us he looked at his disciples and said, "You are those who have stayed with me in my trials" (Luke 22:28). Interestingly, this passage suggests that Jesus did entrust himself to people. At first glance, it seems like there is a contradiction between these verses, but there is quite a difference in relationship equity between these two scenes. One scene is comprised of a crowd of consumers loitering to see the big show of Jesus's ministry. But these people aren't in the trenches of ministry with Jesus as the disciples were. No, the passage in Luke 22 is addressed to a small group of men whom Jesus knew personally. So Jesus did entrust himself to people within a community context, knowing full well that Peter would deny him, Thomas would doubt his resurrection, and all would scatter from the scene of Jesus's arrest in the garden.

The lesson here is twofold: we entrust ourselves to others with discernment. Just because a ministry draws a crowd doesn't mean every person is on Jesus's mission. Second, we cannot entrust ourselves to others under a conviction that they won't hurt us; rather, we entrust ourselves out of love for them. Jesus learned to live in loving community with his disciples so much so that he called them his family (Matt. 12:46–50).

There are many things we can observe about Jesus's living in community with his disciples:

- They pray (Luke 11:1–4).
- They minister (Matt. 14:13–21).
- They debrief their ministry experiences (Mark 9:28–29).
- They challenge one another (Matt. 16:21–23).
- They get frustrated with one another (Mark 9:33–34).
- They love one another (John 13:34–35).

Jesus, the God-man, is the only person who has ever perfectly imaged God as both God and man, and yet he chose not to go it alone. Instead he invites imperfect disciples to walk with him. Jesus knew it isn't good for man to be alone; an isolated man diminishes the grandeur of imaging God. How could it be any other way if there isn't another person there to behold God being imaged? Could this be why Jesus was so disheartened by Philip's comment in John 14:8, "Lord, show us the Father, and it is enough for us"? Jesus said to him, "Have I been with you so long, and you still do not know me, Philip? Whoever has seen me has seen the Father. How can you say, 'Show us the Father'?" (v. 9). You see, Jesus was already perfectly imaging the Father and yet Philip completely missed the point. Jesus is described as "the radiance of the glory of God and the exact imprint of his nature" (Heb. 1:3) and as "the image of the invisible God" (Col. 1:15).

Jesus Imaged God and Lived in Community

You and I must live in community if we want to walk as Jesus did (1 John 2:6) and if we want to experience and express imaging God to others. Jesus not only shared his life with others, but he also shared his ministry with others. Luke 9 has a description of Jesus commissioning the Twelve to proclaim the gospel. In Luke

10, he appoints and deploys seventy-two additional followers to share in the story line of rebuilding his kingdom. It is one thing to minister to one another in community, but it is quite another to do ministry as community, sharing mission, upholding each other, encouraging the discouraged, and rejoicing with the fruitful (even if or when you personally are not). This kind of gospel kinship is what was lost in the fall, when man was completely alienated (from God, others, and self). Jesus is the pathway to reconciliation on every front (Rom. 5:10–11). He then, in turn, commissions us as his followers to share in his ministry of reconciliation (2 Cor. 5:18–19).

Missional Living

Jesus stayed in constant contact with the Father (John 5:19–20), which is how he was able to keep his eye on the mission. In the midst of experiencing intimacy with God, gaining identity from imaging God, and the joy of community, it is only a consuming love of God that would compel someone to think about others (friends and enemies alike). Many people do not experience the joy, love, and fulfillment that is found in the gospel. Some of them may mock you for being a Christ follower. Yet Jesus lived and died with these very people on his mind.

Consider a really amazing day in the life of Jesus, which is found in Mark 1. Jesus came to a synagogue and taught the Scriptures. People were amazed at his teaching. During his teaching time, a demon disrupted his lesson. Jesus confronted the demon and commanded it to leave, and again people were amazed. Ready for some downtime, Jesus headed over to Peter's house, only to find Peter's mother-in-law sick with a fever. Jesus healed this woman, and she got up and prepared lunch. By sunset, the entire town had gathered at Peter's house; the crowd sprawled out past the front doors and spilled into the street. The crowd was composed not just of the curious but also of the sick and demon-possessed. Jesus did not send them away or retreat but healed

1. whole story
2. prayer, solitude
3. story

them, well into the night. Then, in the early hours before dawn, he retreated to a solitary place to pray. These habits of prayer and solitude are how Jesus gained perspective, heard from the Father, and stayed aligned to the mission given him by the Father.

His disciples found him, and Peter asked him why he was out there, saying, "Everyone is looking for you" (v. 37). Peter was probably thinking, "This is it, our big break. We can set up a ministry center, and people will come from all around." So Jesus said to his disciples, in essence, "Let's pack up. We must be going. It is the nature of our mission that we must go to those who are not experiencing the life-giving impact of redemptive community" (v. 38). So, they went from village to village proclaiming the good news, the story of God.

Think of the ways mission could have been abandoned in just this one day in Jesus's life:

- The argument of fruitfulness: "You can't leave now; we are just starting to make an impact here."
- The argument of need: "What will these people do if we leave them?"
- The argument of opportunity: "Why should we go somewhere that may not be as open to the gospel? If we don't strike while the iron is hot, we're going to miss this opportunity."

Jesus centered himself effectively on the Father's call upon his life: "to seek and to save the lost" (Luke 19:10). He would not settle for the fruitless characteristics of religious leaders (Matt. 23:23, 25–28). He had a heart for lost people (Luke 10:2), and it drove him to order his life in such a way that people had to figure out what to do with him (Matt. 16:13–18). This model of intersecting lives and culture, of getting in the way relationally, was established for us by Jesus. *If we are to follow him, we must follow him as redeemed image bearers, as worshipers, as a community, and as missionaries.*

Look at one more example, in Mark 5:1–20, where Jesus

delivered a man from demonic torment. This man experienced redemption and begged to follow Jesus. Then Jesus invited the man to give his life to telling people the great things God had done for him, but not as part of Jesus's team. He was commissioned by Jesus to go to his hometown, in the Decapolis region, and tell its residents what God had done for him. Matthew tells us Jesus ministered in this area and was very fruitful (Matt. 4:25). So we see that Jesus shared his ministry with this man by allowing him to prepare hearts for the message that Jesus would later come to proclaim. Can you see a pattern emerging? He restored this man from image distorter to image bearer; the man was able to worship God within his culture and context, and others were brought into the redemptive story through the man's role in God's story.

It becomes clear: Jesus is the hero of God's story. He is also the way you and I get a sweet part in the story. Without Jesus's death, burial, resurrection, and ascension from where he intercedes on our behalf, we are left to live a life marred by sin, distorting the God of the story as we image him. Even after our redemption, we are not left on our own to do our best to image God; he comes to our rescue (Matt. 28:19–20) and makes us new creatures in his likeness (Eph. 4:17–24) and in his image (Col. 3:5–10), and we are being renewed in his image from one degree of glory to another (2 Cor. 3:18). This reconciliation allows us to rightly respond to him.

Perhaps you've experienced something like this: you're sitting alone, waiting for a friend in a public gathering place. The busyness of the crowd—buying lattes and jockeying for tables and chairs amidst loud conversations, spills, strollers, and cell phones—is overstimulating. Someone with an audience-commanding presence walks by and smiles, so you smile in return. He gives a nod or a wave, and you give a nod or a wave; then he says hello, and just before you reply, you hear a voice behind you saying hello. You were responding to him, but all the while his attention was locked on someone behind you.

This experience is a bit how it can be to live as worshipers once Jesus has established a saving relationship with us. We continue to live in a world of people, opportunities, fortunes, and misfortunes, but in the midst of it all, we fix our gaze on Jesus (Heb. 12:1–3), not on our environment. Doing so allows us to act inappropriately or free from our circumstances. We go through a trial and can count it joy (James 1:2–3). When we find ourselves in mourning, we consider ourselves among the blessed (Matt. 5:4). We find ourselves in the celebration rhythms of life— births and weddings—and we praise the giver of all good things (1 Thess. 5:18). We are able to have a worshiper's response because we have an awe-inspiring focal point. When we are able to see Jesus across the crowd, behind the veneer of success, and in the eyes of others, we will have inappropriate responses to circumstances that require an explanation for the hope that is within us (1 Pet. 3:15).

So we see in Jesus a template of what an image bearer's life looks like, yet he did much more than leave us a morally inspiring life. He paid the price for our sin by dying on the cross, and he champions the way for our redemption through his resurrection. He began a disciple-making movement that carries on to this day. Jesus makes it possible for his disciples (then and now) to reach their world through him. Jesus is the premier example of a disciple, but he is also the premier example of a disciple-maker. When he ascended into heaven, he left behind a band of transformed and transforming men who turned their world upside down by how they lived and how Jesus lived through them.

In our everyday world, our part in the story of God is to live in such a way that others would see and experience the transforming work and presence of Jesus. When this is done, we are not merely those in the story. We become God's way of sharing his story and inviting others into their roles within his story.

CHAPTER 2 ASSIGNMENT

Encounter the Hero of the Story

In this assignment you will look at experiences and descriptions of Jesus. Imagine being there, hearing Jesus say these words, seeing the vision John saw, or reading the words Paul penned. What would it be like if your life were so consumed with Jesus that you used all of it to declare him the hero of God's story?

1) How does John the Baptist describe Jesus? How does the Father describe Jesus? (Matthew 3)
2) How does John describe Jesus in Revelation 1?
3) What does Jesus claim about himself in John 8:31–59?
4) How does Jesus handle temptation? (Matt. 4:1–11)
5) Using Paul's outline of love (1 Cor. 13:4–8), search the Gospel of Mark for how Jesus displays love.

Digging Deeper

Explore Jesus through the names God reveals through his Word.

Advocate (1 John 2:1)
Almighty (Matt. 28:18; Rev. 1:8)
Alpha and Omega (Rev. 1:8; 22:13)
Amen (Rev. 3:14)
Apostle of our confession (Heb. 3:1)
Author of life (Acts 3:15)
Beginning and end (Rev. 22:13)
Beginning of God's creation (Rev. 3:14)
Blessed and only Sovereign (1 Tim. 6:15)
Bread of God (John 6:33)
Bread of life (John 6:35; 6:48)
Cornerstone (Acts 4:11; Eph. 2:20; 1 Pet. 2:7)
Chief Shepherd (1 Pet. 5:4)
Christ (1 John 2:22)
Creator (John 1:3)

Deliverer (Rom. 11:26)

Door (John 10:9)

Eternal life (1 John 1:2; 5:20)

Everlasting Father (Isa. 9:6)

Faithful and True (Rev. 19:11)

Faithful witness (Rev. 1:5)

Faithful and true witness (Rev. 3:14)

First and last (Rev. 1:17; 2:8; 22:13)

Firstborn of the dead (Rev. 1:5)

Founder and perfecter of our faith (Heb. 12:2)

Founder of salvation (Heb. 2:10)

God (John 1:1; 20:28; Heb. 1:8; Rom. 9:5; 2 Pet. 1:1; 1 John 5:20)

Good shepherd (John 10:11, 14)

Great shepherd (Heb. 13:20)

Great high priest (Heb. 4:14)

Head of the church (Eph. 1:22; 4:15; 5:23)

Heir of all things (Heb. 1:2)

High priest (Heb. 2:17)

Holy and Righteous One (Acts 3:14)

Holy and true one (Rev. 3:7)

Hope (1 Tim. 1:1)

Hope of glory (Col. 1:27)

Horn of salvation (Luke 1:69)

I am (John 8:58)

Image of God (2 Cor. 4:4)

King of ages (1 Tim. 1:17)

King of Israel (John 1:49)

King of the Jews (Matt. 27:11)

King of kings (1 Tim 6:15; Rev. 19:16)

King of the nations (Rev. 15:3)

Lamb (Rev. 13:8)

Lamb of God (John 1:29)

Lamb without blemish (1 Pet. 1:19)

Last Adam (1 Cor. 15:45)

Life (John 14:6; Col. 3:4)

Light of the world (John 8:12)

Lion of the tribe of Judah (Rev. 5:5)

Living one (Rev. 1:18)

Living stone (1 Pet. 2:4)

Lord (2 Pet. 2:20)

Lord of all (Acts 10:36)

Lord of glory (1 Cor. 2:8)

Lord of lords (Rev. 19:16)

Lord [YHWH] our righteousness (Jer. 23:6)

Man of heaven (1 Cor. 15:48)

Master (Luke 5:5; 8:24; 9:33)

Mediator of a new covenant (Heb. 9:15)

Mighty God (Isa. 9:6)

Morning star (Rev. 22:16)

Only Son (John 1:18; 1 John 4:9)

Our great God and Savior (Titus 2:13)

Our guard (2 Thess. 3:3)

Our husband (2 Cor. 11:2)

Our redemption (1 Cor. 1:30)

Our righteousness (1 Cor. 1:30)

Our sacrificed Passover lamb (1 Cor. 5:7)

Our sanctification (1 Cor. 1:30)

Power of God (1 Cor. 1:24)

Precious cornerstone (1 Pet. 2:6)

Prince of Peace (Isa. 9:6)

Prophet (Acts 3:22)

Propitiation for our sins (1 John 2:2)

Resurrection and life (John 11:25)

Righteous Branch (Jer. 23:5)

Righteous One (Acts 7:52; 1 John 2:1)

Rock (1 Cor. 10:4)

Root of David (Rev. 5:5; 22:16)

Ruler of the kings on earth (Rev. 1:5)

Savior (Eph. 5:23; Titus 1:4; 3:6; 2 Pet. 2:20)

Son of David (Luke 18:39)

Son of God (John 1:49; Heb. 4:14)

Son of Man (Matt. 8:20)

Son of the Most High (Luke 1:32)
Source of eternal salvation to all who obey him (Heb. 5:9)
The one mediator (1 Tim. 2:5)
The stone that was rejected (Acts 4:11)
True bread (John 6:32)
True light (John 1:9)
True vine (John 15:1)
Truth (John 1:14; 14:6)
Way (John 14:6)
Wisdom of God (1 Cor. 1:24)
Wonderful Counselor (Isa. 9:6)
Word (John 1:1)
Word of God (Rev. 19:13)

3

IMAGE

I sat by the side of the bed and watched as my wife labored for breath, fading in and out of consciousness. For days she had been bedridden; for months she had been declining in strength and health. We talked about the many people who had come to visit for the last time. We rejoiced that she had lived to see our oldest daughter marry just three months before. We looked at pictures from ministry trips and vacations around the globe—Czech Republic, Spain, France, Mexico, Hawaii.

In her moments of unconsciousness I asked God, "Show me the value of human life; show me how this unconscious woman glorifies you." The phrase that came to my mind was, "I am pleased with her." The more I thought about it, I was reminded of how God the Father relates to his Son and to us: "This is my beloved Son, with whom I am well pleased" (Matt. 3:17); and, "In love he predestined us for adoption as sons through Jesus Christ, according to the purpose of his will, to the praise of his glorious grace, with which he has blessed us in the Beloved" (Eph. 1:4–6). I realized how very *me-centered* and *man-centered* I was: unless this made sense to me, unless it was pleasing to me, and unless it fit a purpose of my will, then my wife's cancer was certainly not the best God could be doing.

My wife, in a video interview used during a Mars Hill Church service, said that she had given her life to God and that he had the right to do with it what he wanted. My question to God had way more to do with "Why don't you want to do more with her?"

That was my struggle with God. "Isn't there *more* than imaging him or more than pleasing him?" The answer is no. He has designed and redeemed us to be image bearers, which has to do with relationship. "God has placed man into a threefold relationship: between man and God, between man and his fellowmen, and between man and nature."[1] Our value in God's eyes is not determined by what we can do above and beyond his design for us but in the inherent nature of how we function in relationship to him, others, and his creation. It is our relationships that truly bear the image of God.

The Image of God Is Common to All Humans

I thought of the men I know and have known—pastors, teachers, seminary presidents, ministry executives, missionaries, evangelists—and I thought that the greatest thing they could do at any moment in their life is to please God. No amount of fruitfulness, obedience, productivity, or over-the-top performance could trump simply pleasing God. So, I sat beside the bed of my wife of thirty years as she lay there finishing well and pleasing God.

The image of God is a quality, a characteristic, an attribute, a function, and a relational capacity that allows a human to image God in a way that pleases and glorifies him. The Bible is not precise or definitive as to what the *image of God* is, yet God is clear in his Word that every human is an image bearer. The capacity to bear his image in some distorted way survived the sinful fall of mankind. Anthony Hoekema sums up the biblical understanding:

> So, to be faithful to the biblical evidence, our understanding of the image of God must include these two senses: (1) The image of God as such is an unlosable aspect of man, a part of his essence and existence, something that man cannot lose without ceasing to be man. (2) The image of God, however, must also be understood as that likeness to God which was perverted when

man fell into sin, and is being restored and renewed in the process of sanctification.[2]

Male and female are said to be created in the image and likeness of God (Gen. 1:26–27). Consider the rationale of murder as a capital offense. It is the taking of human life; therefore, it is the destruction of a divine image bearer (Gen. 9:5–6). James 3:9–10 speaks of an untamable tongue that blesses God while cursing humans made in his likeness. Obviously, Genesis 9 and James 3 address people in a post-fall condition, yet we possess some value-giving vestige of God's original design as image bearers. Paul tells his readers to "put on the new self, which is being renewed in knowledge after the image of its creator" (Col. 3:10). This verse demonstrates that while the image of God may have indeed survived the explosive bombardment of sin into the spiritual DNA of humans, it is in need of radical refurbishing or restoration.

To complicate the matter further, Paul does not say that this image *is* renewed, but rather that it is *being* renewed. This means that God's renewal project is in process. Hoekema explains that "the new selves believers have put on are not yet perfect or sinless, since these new selves must still be progressively renewed by the Holy Spirit. Christians should therefore see themselves as people who are genuinely new, though not yet totally new."[3] It is not a one-time event or transaction; it is a continual transaction, and this work of God continues in our lives until it is complete (Phil. 1:6).

This understanding is what Paul has in mind when he says, "For now we see in a mirror dimly, but then face to face. Now I know in part; then I shall know fully, even as I have been fully known" (1 Cor. 13:12). Paul was longing for the day when imaging will be exact and not distorted. This work of God in remaking us in Christ into the image of God is our gospel identity, and our hope of it completed is a consequence of God's sharing his story with us.

Image Bearers Are Valuable

While I was growing up, the same assault was mounted upon our school every year—the standardized Scholastic Aptitude Test. We were each given a Scantron answer sheet and booklet. We were strictly forbidden to begin or proceed to the next sections without permission. The part of this drill I never questioned was the writing instrument— a No. 2 pencil. We were always told to use a No. 2 pencil. I never thought my answers could be more impressive if I used a No. 1 pencil. I never wondered how many pencil numbers there were, or even what the numbers meant. I didn't realize that the numbers referred to the hardness or softness of the lead (the lower the number, the softer the lead. For some reason, the No. 2 pencil was the preferred instrument for this annual trauma.

My take-away from the annual ordeal was this: humans are designed to be *number-two priorities of life*. The *number-one priority* is to be God. But humans rebel at the notion of being instruments with a number-two value. We think that a number-two being cannot possibly be the best instrument with which to complete the test called "My Life." We desire—no, crave—to be number one, and when we make our marks as number one, they are too faint to be read. As gods we fail miserably. As image bearers of God, however, we have been designed for lives of profound meaning. Humans are designed to image or reflect God their Creator (Gen. 1:26–27). Don't let the subtlety of this escape you. Our design as humans inherently requires something to image—God.

I am amazed at how many useless inventions or products line the shelves of the average store: pour spouts for bottles, kits for marking a straight line on a round golf ball, bookmarks with reading lamps. I am even more amazed at how many useless items sit on my desk as I write: trays to stack paper, a container that looks a lot like a mug but is designed to hold pens and pencils. Expressions abound about useless things and inappropriate applications in which useful things would be useless, for example, a mirror in a world where everyone is blind. What would be the point? No one could see his reflection; no one could see anything reflected in or by the mirror. In fact, no one could see the mirror. The reason that mirrors are useful in our world is that there are sighted observers. Just so, the reason that image bearers are valued in God's world is that he is pleased when imaged, and pleasing him is the most profound activity a human can do. God further uses his image bearers to reflect himself to other observers, our fellow humans (as part of his gospel story) and angels.[4]

"Image of God" is a meaningless description without a God to image. What's worse is when people miss the point that they are God's image bearers and elevate being human as an ultimate calling. To leave God out of the picture means to sabotage our chance to image him. And when we don't image him, by default we image ourselves and elevate ourselves as god. This is the height of idolatry. Our frame of reference is too small in our self-centeredness, our limited perspectives, and our limited resources. When we live life from this limited human point of view, it's inevitable that we produce faint, distorted versions of God instead of the person and love of God.

A woman in her twenties came to talk with me and asked, "Why don't relationships work out for me?" Her relationship struggles were a recurring problem. She lived in an emotional ghetto called "romance." The woman who choked out this question between sobs believes every guy she meets is "the one." She doesn't say, "He might be the one"; she goes all in from the first casual interaction to the final painful silence of abandonment. She wonders how things could have begun so well and ended so badly, and why guys who have so much in their favor can be so clueless in their interactions with women.

I asked her, "Have you ever asked yourself why, when you jump in the water, it seems to scare away the fish?" She answered, "Oh, yeah, all the time." From there we considered where she gets her sense of value and meaning. Though the options seemed many, we came to a recurring and heartbreaking answer: "I feel most alive when someone is paying attention to me."

Unfortunately, this same conversation happens frequently in counseling sessions. It is representative of a people with a tribal-like identity centered in romance. One young woman told me that she feared getting out of bed because she feared that, if she got up, the man next to her wouldn't care if she left. My heart broke to hear a woman tell me she would rather be used than ignored.

Such women are not mirrors reflecting the image of the God who declares them valuable; they become movie screens onto which men project their devaluing thoughts and sensuality.

Can you glimpse the vacuum of such souls? They would rather be anything, even dehumanized objects, than nothing. Such is the experience of an image bearer who bears only empty images. We humans fail to grasp that we are most human when we image God. We vainly seek an image of our own to bear, hoping to project a self-image so captivating that others will love and accept us.

Peter makes this appeal to women: "Let your adorning be the hidden person of the heart with the imperishable beauty of a gentle and quiet spirit, which in God's sight is very precious" (1 Pet. 3:4). Peter calls women to trust the original design by encouraging them to believe that God's pleasure matters most. Imaging God to others is valuable to God. Being number two and letting God be number one is a tremendous act of faith. In fact, it involves our whole identity being wrapped up in the person of our Creator. How would this impact someone living in the romance ghetto? The strength that comes from imaging God allows her to go reality TV rather than Disney. She does not have to mentally project herself to a final ballroom dance and a relationship-binding kiss; she can have fun over a latte or some teriyaki, and if the dude never calls again, she is no less valuable. She is free and complete in her identity as an image bearer of God.

A Mystery

As image bearers we are a mystery. I am constantly surprised by the people I meet who want to know the secret, the thing, or the magical technique that can turn their life or family around. I don't know why it surprises me. I have been on this Christian journey for over forty years, and I still lapse into desiring a formula fix. More than once I have ministered with formula-oriented disciple makers. One such colleague was a classic. He used the same lessons, verses, and reading materials for everyone he discipled. He believed that his discipleship method was successful because many people had completed it, and it was exponential because several of those he had discipled were now taking others through the same lessons. When I asked him about his disciples' abilities to navigate difficult territory—such as a spouse who just wants to "get wild" for a while, or a deacon who absconds with funds from the church, or their own habitual sin that, if confessed publicly, could forfeit their ministry—my friend's answer was, "Bill, I am just trying to get these guys through the basics." My questions have more to do with what *are* the basics.

Unfortunately, my friend saw moral behavior as the benchmark of maturity. I believe people will see their life take on the fruit of the Spirit (Gal. 5:22–23), but I also believe there are many people who have a form of godliness but know little if anything of the transforming work of the Holy Spirit. Sadly, my friend's church splintered, and he moved on to a more established church that was able to appreciate the need for his idea of discipleship.

The point I am attempting to make is that if someone is oriented toward imaging God, then the disciple-making process will be more transformational than an informational set of verses and lessons. It is not my intention to disrespect my friend, but

I don't see how teaching people that they are image bearers of God and asking the question, "How will this action or attitude image or distort the God of the Bible?" could be more basic to the nature of living as followers of Jesus. This perspective has to be our baseline (1 John 2:6).

Designed for Wonder

As creations in the image of God we are designed for wonder. Not only are we a mystery, but every consideration of God on our behalf gets extrapolated to mystery, as well. That God loves us, not for anything inherent within us, is a mystery. That God has a sovereign plan and holds us responsible for the life choices we make is a mystery. That God has the power to do whatever delights him, yet in his created world realities exist that grieve him, is a mystery. It is beyond us that God would consider us at all.

In chapters 38 through 41 of the book of Job, God asks Job over sixty questions about the governance of his creation. The point of this inquisition was to provoke awe, humble submission, and wonder. God was calling Job out on his thinking that God owed him an explanation for the downturn in his life. The expected response from Job was worship, just as he had responded when he received reports that amounted to the worst day of his life.[5]

Perhaps the greatest response to wonder is gratitude. The most common assignment I find myself giving to those I counsel is to journal what's right with the world every day for a week. I am amazed at how set we have become on what's wrong with our lives, and it causes us to lose our sense of wonder, which in turn, undermines our lives as grateful worshipers. Paul Miller puts it this way: "Cynicism looks reality in the face, calls it phony, and prides itself on its insight as it pulls back. Thanksgiving looks reality in the face and rejoices at God's care."[6]

A couple came to see me. They were amazingly bright people,

and between them they had amassed five graduate degrees. The husband, John, had just finished his second master's degree and was looking for a job. At the time, his wife, Helen, was working and commanding a wage that allowed them to live quite well. John would begin his day by making a few inquiries about elegant jobs and then get busy on projects around the house. These were mega projects such as installing hardwood floors, refinishing kitchen cabinets, and replacing old windows with newer double-glazed panes. When his wife came home, she was met regularly with a litany of wrongs. She hadn't bought the right cottage cheese, and she had neglected to notice that one of the cabinet doors had been hung or that a window frame had been stained. It wasn't as though John didn't love Helen; it was that nothing was right with John's world. When Helen wasn't home, he complained to himself about the ridiculous job-hunting process he was being subjected to and how his degrees seemed worthless. If he had known the economy was going to take a downturn, he would never have bought their old house. John was imaging the fallen world rather than its Redeemer. When I gave John the journaling assignment, he said, "I will have to live in your world because there isn't anything right in my world."

Imagine Helen, sitting on the couch next to John when he said that there is nothing right in his world. What kind of God is John imaging? John admitted that he was down on life, but John did not admit that he could not make a better world. John is convinced that he could improve on God's design. Job came dangerously close to thinking the same way, and God dosed him with questions designed to restart the fire of wonder, calling him to his rightful role of worshiper.

Later we will look at the dynamic of worship and idolatry, but here it is crucial that we understand the implications of imaging God back to God. We, as worshipers, are designed to respond to who God is and what he does. I love this description of worship by William Temple, the archbishop of Canterbury (1942–1944):

Worship is the submission of all of our nature to God.
It is the quickening of conscience by His holiness,
Nourishment of mind by His truth,
Purifying of imagination by His beauty,
Opening of the heart to His love,
And submission of will to his purpose.
And all this gathered up in adoration is the greatest of human
expressions of which we are capable.

Living a wonder-filled life is what it looks like to bear the image of the God of wonder.

Interconnected Imagers of God

I have lived much of my life as a *rescuer*. I wasn't familiar with the term or its characteristics until sometime after I had begun to experience some of its dysfunction. In some dysfunctional relationships there are three players: an oppressor, a victim, and a rescuer. Codependency occurs when a victim needs someone to oppress him or her, and a rescuer needs someone to rescue from oppression. If I am a rescuer, I find myself connecting with someone in trouble in order to find my identity. To get out of rescuer mode has been a painful extraction for me. An even harder dimension has been to learn how to stay compassionate and helpful to someone without trying to be his or her functional savior. Doing so is the fine art or life skill of living well in community.

I have several rescuer friends who are becoming skeptical of community. They wonder if people call them only because they need something. They don't seem to be able to trust that image bearing is significant enough to distinguish them in a world of achievement. Often, their work becomes their identity. The too many hours they spend at work reflect their character of *heart*; their earnings image their *strength*; their decision-making ability shows their agile *mind*; and their teams seem so motivated and productive by the ethos or *soul* they bring to the

table. I have described them this way to correspond to the Great
Commandment. Jesus congratulated a lawyer for knowing God's
priority for life:

> And behold, a lawyer stood up to put him to the test, saying,
> "Teacher, what shall I do to inherit eternal life?" He said to
> him, "What is written in the Law? How do you read it?" And
> he answered, "You shall love the Lord your God with all your
> *heart* and with all your *soul* and with all your *strength* and with
> all your *mind*, and your neighbor as yourself." And he said to
> him, "You have answered correctly; do this, and you will live."
> (Luke 10:25–28)

Can you see how easily "image drift" can set in? What are
originally thought to be blessings from God—raises, promo-
tions, positions, and possessions—slowly edge their way into
the very place where God is to be imaged. Several of my rescuer
friends feel used when someone calls with a need, yet putting
themselves in the position to meet the need has become part
of their identity. Someone who projects a certain image and
then feels used for what that image seems to offer suffers the
great pain of emptiness. This tragedy is seen in many stories
of people being used. Many Christians talk about God's using
them, and in one sense it truly is thrilling to sense God actually
working through our words and resources to impact another.
I wish there was another word for it, though, because no one
really wants to be used. We want to be useful, but ultimately,
we would rather be loved.

Our possessions and our talents are more like a lower-
numbered pencil, which is best used for shading and artistic
design, than for imaging God or our identity. Paul described the
role of creation in representing its Creator:

> For the wrath of God is revealed from heaven against all ungod-
> liness and unrighteousness of men, who by their unrighteous-
> ness suppress the truth. For what can be known about God is

plain to them, because God has shown it to them. For his invisible attributes, namely, his eternal power and divine nature, have been clearly perceived, ever since the creation of the world, in the things that have been made. So they are without excuse. For although they knew God, they did not honor him as God or give thanks to him, but they became futile in their thinking, and their foolish hearts were darkened. Claiming to be wise, they became fools, and exchanged the glory of the immortal God for images resembling mortal man and birds and animals and creeping things. (Rom. 1:18–23)

In verse 20 Paul says that God's invisible attributes, his eternal power and divine nature, are clearly perceived in nature. God has gone way beyond revealing power in designing image bearers. We get the opportunity to demonstrate unmerited love to a baby who has done nothing but breathe and make messes. We get to forgive people who have neither asked for it nor deserved it. We get to grace people by treating them with dignity. Without personal connection we miss the imaging opportunity of portraying a personal God.

Look at the first and last phrases of Psalm 98:

Oh sing to the LORD a new song,
    for he has done marvelous things!
His right hand and his holy arm
    have worked salvation for him.
The LORD has made known his salvation;
    he has revealed his righteousness in the sight of the nations.
He has remembered his steadfast love and faithfulness
    to the house of Israel.
All the ends of the earth have seen
    the salvation of our God. . . .
Let the sea roar, and all that fills it;
    the world and those who dwell in it!
Let the rivers clap their hands;
    let the hills sing for joy together
before the LORD, for he comes
    to judge the earth.

He will judge the world with righteousness,
and the peoples with equity. (Ps. 98:1-3, 7-9)

Nature is given poetic description in the psalm. Seas roar, rivers clap their hands, and hills sing, but the masterpiece is God's saving his people. The true celebration is in the restoring of an image bearer who reflects the steadfast love, faithfulness, righteousness, and justice of his God. This means that for us to function as a mirror in which someone else can see God, we must see ourselves as interconnected, as living in community.

Imaging God to a Broken World

Community—this word has recently made my list of overused and most misunderstood words. I drive by buildings being erected in Seattle over which hang banners that read, "Coming soon: a new urban community." Some time ago I drove by an undeveloped subdivision in Illinois that advertised "A new traditional community." When I speak of community, I am speaking of relationships and the quality of those relationships. These relationships will extend to geography, affinity, and those we work with. We all have a desire to belong, so much so that it may even be part of the image of God. Finding ways to experience and express belonging to those not yet part of our faith community is what we call "mission."

- John 3:16 tells us, "God so loved the world, that he gave his only Son."
- Romans 5:8 tells us, "While we were still sinners, Christ died for us."
- Romans 5:10 calls us God's enemies: "While we were enemies we were reconciled to God."

As we have seen before, God's mission is one of reconciliation. Paul saw himself and other believers as ambassadors of reconciliation (2 Cor. 5:20). This is what it looks like to image God to those who are not part of the community of faith. So let's loop this chapter back on itself. We started by saying everyone images God to one degree of distortion or another. If this is true, then being on mission may not be about what help you can offer as much as about partnering with unbelieving image bearers already imaging (although distorted) the God they don't know.

When I was planting a church, I did some inquiries into that neighborhood to find needs that we as a church could help meet. Several people involved in the church plant wanted to start a food closet, but we found that the food bank in our neighborhood was doing an exceptional job and was raising funds for a new facility. One of the people in our church called the food bank and asked how we could be of help. We were told that over 60 percent of the clients at the food bank were single mothers who were regularly in need of disposable diapers. We decided to give the food bank a couple hundred dollars each month for diapers and to ask our members to serve at the neighborhood food bank, rather than open our own food closet. About a year later, we hosted a fundraising banquet for the food bank, and I was asked to share the story of our church. I related how we partner with the food bank, and a couple of weeks later I had several community business people talking to me about spiritual things. Within the next year, I was a member of the leadership team for the chamber of commerce. I have had more than a few profoundly spiritual conversations through these venues. These opportunities came from finding ways that God was already being imaged (distorted or not) and joining my fellow image bearers in looking for ways to further image him.

Gospel identity for us lies in having a renewed image as imagers of God. Through the work of the Holy Spirit, God allows himself to be seen by us and through us. He graces us with letting us be part of his story. To try and hijack the story from God or take the lead role away from Jesus is to act less like a human and more like the things of which men make idols.

CHAPTER 3 ASSIGNMENT

Exposing Yourself to Your Calling as an Image Bearer

Look at the following verses with a view toward sensing the genius and wonder God displayed in creating beings who could image him without being him. As you work through these verses, ask God to give you an appreciation for your high calling as a bearer of his image.

1) Read Genesis 1:26–27. What do you think God had in mind when he designed humans as his image bearers?
2) Read Genesis 3:1–6. How was God's image distorted rather than reflected in the garden?
3) Read Colossians 3:1–17. What hope does Paul give to image bearers?
4) Read Psalm 23. What role does God play in our walking with him?
5) Read John 15:1–17. What does a fruitful person look like?

Digging Deeper

God did for you each of the things below the moment you became a Christian. As you work through this list, take the time to thank God, as well as declare them as truth statements God says about you. How does this list speak to your identity in Jesus?

Thirty-One Things That Happen at Salvation[7]

You are redeemed from slavery to sin (Rom. 3:24; 8:23)

You are reconciled to God (2 Cor. 5:18–20)

You are forgiven for all your sins (Col. 2:13)

You are freed from the law of sin and death (Rom. 6:14; 8:1–4; Gal. 5:1–4)

You are adopted by God (Gal. 3:26–4:7; Eph. 1:4–5)

You become a child of God (John 3:3, 7)

You are accepted by God (Eph. 1:6)

You are justified by Jesus Christ (Romans 4; 5:1)

You are glorified with Jesus (Rom. 4:16–17; 8:30; Col. 3:4)

You are united to Jesus (Col. 2:9–10)

You possess every spiritual blessing (Eph. 1:3)

You are brought close to God (Eph. 2:13)

You are delivered from the power of darkness (2 Cor. 4:3–4; Col. 1:13)

You are transferred from Satan's domain to the kingdom of God (Col. 1:13; 1 Thess. 2:12)

You are given as a gift (John 17)

You are circumcised in Christ (Col. 2:11)

You join the priesthood of believers (1 Pet. 2:5; Rev. 1:6)

You join the people of God (1 Pet. 2:9)

You receive citizenship in heaven (Eph. 2:19; Phil. 3:20)

You are a member of the family of God (Gal. 6:10; Eph. 2:19)

You take up the fellowship of the saints (John 17:11–23; Eph. 4:1–3)

You are granted access to God (Heb. 4:16; 10:10–20)

You become an inheritance (Eph. 1:6, 18)

You receive an inheritance (Eph. 1:14; Col. 3:24; 1 Pet. 1:4; Heb. 9:15)

You become as light to the world (Eph. 5:8)

You are in God (1 Thess. 1:1)

God the Father is in you (Eph. 4:6)

You are in the Son (Rom. 8:1)

The Son is in you (John 14:20)

You are in the Spirit (Rom. 8:9)

The Spirit is in you (1 Cor. 2:12)

4

IDENTITY DISTORTIONS

I have a friend who decided to do a bonding sort of project with his teenage son—restore an old Chevy Camaro. The project started with finding an old worse-for-wear car, then, piece by piece, either restoring or replacing parts. All the parts—seats, transmission, and engine—were collected, then refurbished, and finally assembled. When the car was completed, it was actually better than originally built. A few years went by, and the son decided to sell the car, which at one point became a problem. According to the Washington State Patrol, it was no longer just one car, because it now had a VIN number for the frame, another for the body, and yet another for the engine. The car they had built no longer had the integrity of the original manufacturer.

I have often thought of their car experience in light of how we live our lives. Humans were originally designed to image God, but sin made everyone in need of complete refurbishing. The holy Trinity does a complete restoration project every time someone becomes a Christian. This restoration in Christ actually makes us better than the original, but when we add or subtract to the work of God in Christ, we end up without the integrity of the original manufacturer. "In fact, the very greatness of man's sin consists in the fact that he is still an image-bearer of God," explains Hoekema. "What makes sin so heinous is that man is prostituting such splendid gifts. *Corruptio optimi pessima*: the corruption of the best is the worst."[1] In this chapter, we will look at a few ways in which we distort our identity and in the process distort God as we image him.

Distortion 1: I Am What I Do

You are probably familiar with the practice, which is actually a trap, of describing yourself by what you do: "My name is _____ and I'm a _____" (e.g., Adrian, lawyer). The recovery movement tends to join a person's identity to his enslaving habits: "Hi, my name is _____ and I'm a _____" (e.g., Bill, alcoholic). Let's take a look at more subtle forms of this trap, looking at labels assigned to us over the years by others or ourselves:

- You got glasses, and a classmate called you "four eyes."
- You were overweight, and a coach called you "fatso."
- You were not very coordinated, and you experienced being the leftover after everyone chose teams, and the captain complained that he got stuck with you on his team.

Consider the identity or insecurities you have owned because of failures or shortcomings. Think of all the things you think you can't do. They may include singing, dancing, running a marathon, acting, doing math, writing, or playing an instrument. I have heard it said, "If you want to see a fearless crowd, talk to kids before they start attending school." At that point in their lives, labels haven't stuck, failures haven't hurt, and captains haven't passed over the uncoordinated. Ask those kids if they can play a sport or an instrument, or sing, or dance. They believe they can, because they haven't been wounded yet.

What would it look like to read the Bible with an unwounded heart? To hear God say, "Love your enemy, make disciples, proclaim the gospel, and do the work of the ministry," and to have your first inclination be, "I can do that." God has redeemed us so that we can make this response, because in Christ we are restored. In fact, we are better than new because we are empowered by the Holy Spirit. And just as we saw Jesus being spoken to as being loved before he had performed a miracle or uttered a parable, so you, too, are loved apart from what you do.

I Fail, Therefore I Am

We can easily be tempted to import a therapeutic model for restoring ourselves from our failures or our fears. Brian is such an example. Brian came to see me because he was angry. He knew he should be able to control his temper, but he couldn't. He had walked off his job in a rage, he had broken off his engagement in frustration, and he had cycled through three different community groups because of conflicts with leadership. I asked Brian what he thought his problem was, and he said, "I have a short fuse." Granted, Brian has a short fuse, but that is only a symptom. Brian is frustrated because he wants people to respect him, and he feels that they don't. The truth is that people are quite impressed with Brian, but Brian doesn't know how to handle disagreement, conflict, or even a difference of opinion. To Brian, these feel treasonous. He is threatened and assesses his threat as a lack of respect by others.

The bottom line to Brian's thinking is, "I am what I do, and if people don't like what I do, then they don't like me." Brian's hope, and ours, is in finding identity in the person and work of Jesus. If our identity is so fragile as to depend upon the approval of others, then we will live lives of insecurity, anger, and serial failures. This sort of person is similar to the elder brother in Jesus's parable in Luke 15:11–32:

> Elder brothers have an undercurrent of anger toward life circumstances, hold grudges long and bitterly, look down at people of other races, religions, and lifestyles, experience life as joyless, crushing drudgery, have little intimacy and joy in their prayer lives, and have a deep insecurity that makes them overly sensitive to criticism and rejection yet fierce and merciless in condemning others.[2]

Even if we do achieve greatness in the eyes of many, those stray sniper bullets of disapproval or criticism can rob us of the joy of having helped others.

Judas and Peter

Consider the contrast between Judas and Peter. Judas lived in community with Jesus and the other disciples for three years. He observed the perfect model of love, forgiveness, grace, and mercy—the very incarnation of God himself. Yet Judas found himself stuck in his betrayal of Jesus without the tools to navigate a turnaround. Peter, on the other hand, found himself in a similar circumstance to Judas yet with a radically different outcome. He denied Jesus three times and retreated to weep bitterly (Matt. 26:75). Peter rebounded, however, because he had a redemptive relationship with Jesus, whereas Judas did not. Judas found himself in the painful state called "alone." Peter found himself in the humiliating state called "hypocrite."[3] To be a hypocrite is to live a lie, and Peter's hypocrisy was denying he knew his Lord, Jesus. For Judas, hypocrisy was living as a disciple, deceitfully following Jesus without believing in him or his message.

Here's a time to be introspective: do you find yourself Judas-like, trafficking in a belief culture yet not really sensing you belong? Or are you more like Peter, denying Jesus in order to fit in a culture, when in your heart of hearts you know him to be the Son of God (Matt. 16:16)?

Many people feel that they have played a game-winning hand when they level the hypocrite charge against Christians, and yet Christians who do not understand their identity in Christ do not understand their hypocrisy. It is true—a Christian is often a hypocrite, but not because he is in community, living a life of worship, prayer, and repentance. Hypocrisy for Christians occurs when we sin. Our true identity is as children of God, and it is evidenced when we act like Christ or obey the Scriptures. We are not hypocrites at all; we're authentic. It is in the moments of self-centered living, idolatrous priorities, and bondage to habitual sin that we are acting hypocritical. Yet because these moments feel so natural or are so often our experience, they seem more like our identity, and transformation seems like the act of hypocrisy. Consider how Paul challenges the early church to recalibrate to its new identity in Christ:

- Put on the new self. (Col. 3:12–14)
- You have died. (Col. 3:3)
- It is no longer I who live. (Gal. 2:20)
- Renew your mind. (Rom. 12:1–2)
- Such were some of you. (1 Cor. 6:9–11)

but my past is also my present; same flaws, same repeated mistakes

I Succeed, Therefore I Am

Just as we can mistakenly take on a false identity through our failures or regrets, we can take on a false identity through our successes and achievements. Second Samuel 16–17 tells a tragic story of a man who allowed his identity and role in God's story to become completely distorted. The man's name was Ahithophel, and he had been a key advisor to King David. When Absalom, David's son, attempted a political takeover, David was forced to flee his own palace and capital city, Jerusalem. Ahithophel remained behind and sought to be the royal advisor to Absalom. Ahithophel's counsel was renowned: "The counsel that Ahithophel gave was as if one consulted the word of God; so was all the counsel of Ahithophel esteemed, both by David and by Absalom" (2 Sam. 16:23).

Meanwhile, Hushai, another advisor to the king, persuaded Absalom that Ahithophel's counsel was not sound and should be disregarded. Absalom and his entourage agreed, so they disregarded Ahithophel's counsel (2 Sam. 17:14). Here is a window into a distorted identity. It was no longer meaningful to Ahithophel to deliver God's counsel. He had drifted to the dangerous position of getting his meaning from having his own advice heeded (2 Sam. 17:23).

Ahithophel's advice was sound, but God had a different plotline in his story. God intended to bring harm to Absalom, so God caused Ahithophel's counsel to be disregarded. Ahithophel no longer saw himself as living within the story of God. He had made that oh-so-easy shift to thinking God was in his story. When God moved Absalom to disregard Ahithophel's advice, Ahithophel saw his story going horribly wrong. He didn't trust the bigger arc of God's story and purposes in assessing the situation, so he hanged himself in despair.

Jesus shows us just the opposite response in the garden of Gethsemane. He knew that the life he was living would bring the kingdom of God to earth (Luke 8:1). He knew he was bringing salvation to households (Luke 19:9–10). He knew the Father was pleased with him (Matt. 3:17), so he wrestled time and time again in the garden, surrendering his preferences and justifying God's story line. He came to the empowering resolve that the Father's will (the story of God) is greater than any one scene lived out on earth, even by the story's hero.

The reality is not easy to resolve: "Not my will, but yours, be done" (Luke 22:42). It is the ultimate rite of passage from death of self (Matt. 16:24–25) to experiencing God-given life (John 10:10). Most of us wrestle with the legitimacy of God's having a preset story line, and we experience much drama as we seek to exercise our will. One of the main reasons for such a faith-challenging struggle is that we define *choice* or *free will* as "the ability to determine an outcome between two or more options." We reason, "If God already has the story line established, I must not have a free will." But this is not the model Jesus gave us in the garden (Mark 14:36; Luke 22:42). Jesus did not need the power of contrary choice to join God in his story as a willful participant.[4] Jesus modeled that a surrendered will is a free will. His free choice was to do what he most wanted to do; that is, Jesus most wanted to do what the Father wanted him to do; he surrendered his will to the Father's will.

Envision a hot summer's day. You come in to my ice cream shop near closing time and say, "I'd like an ice cream cone, please." I ask you, "What flavor would you like?" You respond, "Vanilla." I say, "It's a good thing you chose vanilla because it's the only flavor I have left." How do you respond? You might respond, "Well, I didn't really choose a flavor; I merely declared a preference." Or you might say, "It's not much of a choice; I had no options." Or you could say, "I didn't know I had only one option; nevertheless, my choice would have been the same even if every flavor were available to me."

I suggest that entering into God's story as an image bearer means taking the opportunity to image God with our surrendered wills. Our act of loving surrender is a legitimate act of the will, even if it does not determine the outcome of the story. We do not have to be in control of the story line to meaningfully live our role in God's story. In fact, if God were not the one determining the outcome of the story, we would be without a story, and we would be left with "choose your own adventure" vignettes that really tell no story at all. To live as image bearers, refashioned in the image of Christ, looks more like the loving obedience of Jesus in surrender to a grand narrative than like the tragic misread of lost favor before God evidenced in the life of Ahithophel.

Distortion 2: I Am What Has Been Done to Me

A mature Christian woman was pouring herself into a young, single mom named April. The older woman brought April to talk to me. I learned at our first meeting that April had grown up with a passive mother who was a serial lover. Over the years, several of the men in her mother's life had abused April. Her mother's noninvolvement and failure to protect her daughter had a damaging impact upon April. During high school April abused drugs and alcohol. Later, she lived with several men herself. In the midst of all this chaos, she met a guy who was different, and he invited her to his house for dinner, where his family showed her love.

After that evening, April came frequently to their home, and they invited her to church where she made a personal commitment to Jesus. The next year she moved away and before long found herself back in destructive life patterns. During this time, she met another man. They moved in together, had a child, got married, and had several more children. When she came to see me, her husband was in prison for dealing drugs. She is discouraged because no one will hire her. She is also angry because everyone (mother, father, friends, husband, and in-laws) has let her down. She says she doesn't know how to care for her family because she's never been cared for, and when she comes to the end of herself, she medicates with the familiar escapes of alcohol and sex.

Even if you find yourself sharing little in common with April's tragic circumstances, don't miss the blame shifting and identity drift that is all too common. April has been mistreated, abused, and abandoned. What broke my heart as I heard her tell her story was that she had come to believe that what had been done to her was now her identity. She believed she was her tragedies. She had grown so used to living in pain and searching for ways to cope with it that she had forgotten her redeeming encounter with Jesus. Because nothing tangibly good had come of it, she thought it couldn't be real, so reality for her was her harsh world as a victim. Underneath it all was the subtle belief that God owed her more than he was giving her. After all, she had stayed with her husband and done the hard thing of keeping her kids, and she was seeking God. Now, however, God had been added to her list of those who had defrauded her or written her off as worthless.

With an unguarded heart, we will all travel down April's road. We will use the bad things that have happened to us as a way to blame others and legitimize labeling ourselves as victims.

Adam did this with God when confronted with his sin of eating the forbidden fruit. First, it was the woman's fault for offering the fruit to him, and ultimately it was God's fault for giving Adam the woman (Gen. 3:12). April, like each of us, must realize her distorted view of self, God, and his story. April, like most of us, thinks she is entitled to a life where things work out in a way that satisfies her.

The apostle Paul wrote, "I count everything as loss because of the surpassing worth of knowing Christ Jesus my Lord. For his sake I have suffered the loss of all things . . . that I may know him and the power of his resurrection, and may share his sufferings, becoming like him in his death" (Phil. 3:8–10). I used to read these words thinking that whenever I suffered, I was entering more fully into the Christian life, that I was experiencing the cross that every disciple must bear. Paul's words are not about just any suffering; the suffering Jesus experienced was because of someone else's sin. Until I experience being sinned against, I will lack an understanding of the undeserved forgiveness Jesus extends to me.

The apostle Peter says that suffering unjustly is a corridor for experiencing the grace of God (1 Pet. 2:20–23). I am not suggesting that because injustice, malice, and prejudice are just part of the fallen world, we simply have to deal with it. What I am suggesting is that someone other than God has led us to expect a pain-free ride on planet earth. Neither your pain, the wrongs committed against you, impersonal injustices, nor a dehumanizing system has the power or authority to adequately identify you. When you empower them, your identity will always be too small to sustain life. When you harness them, however, by sharing in Christ's suffering, your identity will illustrate to a dazed and confused world that God is all-sufficient to sustain you. God "shouts in our pains: it is his megaphone to rouse a deaf world."[5]

April must see herself as called of God (Eph. 1:4), appointed for God's pleasure (Phil. 2:13), and rescued to do God-ordained good works (Eph. 2:10) if she is going to survive the identity-robbing world in which she lives. As I invited her to enter into community with others, her first words were: "Why? They'll just let me down." I responded, "Of course they will, and you will let them down, but Christian community is about love, forgiveness, and imaging God one to another."

If you find yourself being shaped by the pains and labels of your past, the good news is that the gospel identity Jesus gives allows you to define yourself by the hope and healing he promises rather than by the hurt others have inflicted.

Distortion 3: I Am My Relationships, Roles, and Responsibilities

Consider the following roles or relationships:

- A single thirty-something
- A teenage mom
- A couple unable to have children
- Empty nesters
- A widow
- An engaged woman
- A man married for ten years
- A family of five
- A grandpa
- A foster parent

As the picture of these people comes to mind, can you envision their environment, their emotional or financial conditions? Would you connect emotional words—lonely, angry, loving, happy, worried, wounded, sad, depressed—with the labels above? Given such circumstances (being financially stretched, changing careers, socially isolated, involved in ministry, needing to pay medical bills, medicating with destructive behavior, medicating within socially acceptable bounds), are there roles you might expect to connect with such people? What about spiritual health, which includes consistent time pursuing God, spiritual disciplines, worship, effective witness, compassion for others, life-giving friend-ships, speaking truth, confessing sin, and mercy ministries?

Here's the beauty of having an identity wrapped up in a creator God who exists outside of creation: our identity is "life proof." No matter what circumstances, roles, or responsibilities are added or subtracted to our lives, they do not add to or sub-tract from our identity. Consider Jesus's illustration of contrast in his conclusion to the Sermon on the Mount:

> Everyone then who hears these words of mine and does them will be like a wise man who built his house on the rock. And the rain fell, and the floods came, and the winds blew and beat on that house, but it did not fall, because it had been founded on the rock. And everyone who hears these words of mine and does not do them will be like a foolish man who built his house on the sand. And the rain fell, and the floods came, and the winds blew and beat against that house, and it fell, and great was the fall of it. (Matt. 7:24–27)

A typical Western thinker hears, "If I build my house upon the rock, I will not experience disaster." But the illustration teaches just the opposite: to both the fool and the wise man come wind, rain, and floods. The salient difference is that the man who has built his house upon the rock stands firm. These verses are not saying that life in Jesus is crisis free but, rather, that life in Jesus is crisis proof (Ps. 34:19–21).

Think about it like this: if you shop for a watch and ask the sales clerk, "Is this watch waterproof?" what you mean is, "If I go in the water with this watch on my wrist, will it get ruined?" You do not want to hear, "This watch will run perfectly in a dry environment, so we ask you to keep it from getting wet." I find myself wanting God to give me a crisis- or disaster-free environ-ment rather than wanting to image him without distortion in the depth of crisis. Jesus put himself on the line here, saying, "A life built on me is crisis proof, and I give it an unconditional warranty."

Since this is the case, why do we malfunction in the midst of life's pressure? We do so because Jesus isn't the foundation of our whole lives, and we build our lives on sand. Most Christians are going to say they trust Jesus with the forgiveness of their sins. But they often fail to realize how the gospel informs every facet of their life. Think of it like this: imagine you have a house well over 10,000 square feet built on a 400-square-foot foundation. Now imagine that career, family, and health are additions to the house, but they are not anchored with a strong foundation. What happens when wind and rain come? The sprawling additions of our lives built on sand—such as family, career, or health—are going to sag and eventually collapse.

It is a distortion to think that our identities are defined by our roles, responsibilities, or relationships. Those fortunate enough to experience complete dependence on God for their life and identity join Paul in saying, "Not that I am speaking of being in need, for I have learned in whatever situation I am to be content. I know how to be brought low, and I know how to abound. In any and every circumstance, I have learned the secret of facing plenty and hunger, abundance and need. I can do all things through him who strengthens me" (Phil. 4:11–13).

When we find our identity in Jesus, we become image bearers of the life-giving God of the Bible. We find a source of strength and meaning from being in the story of God. Do you recall how Jesus imaged the Father in how he lived? Jesus is "the exact imprint of his nature" (Heb. 1:3). Jesus, then, is a light source and a window. As a source of light he reveals the divine imprint, letting us see who God is and what God is like. The ways in which the life of Jesus challenges our view of God are insights into our God distortions. As a window, Jesus lets us see humanity as God envisioned it through how he lived— without sin and in right relationship to the Father. Jesus lived the perfect humanity. The next time you think or say, "I'm only human," ask yourself where you got your paradigm of humanity. More than likely, it came less from humanity designed and more from humanity fallen.

So, I am not what I do, but I am what Jesus has done for me. I am a redeemed image bearer, being renewed daily in the image of Christ (Col. 3:10). I am not what has been done to me, but I am free because of what Christ does on my behalf. When I sin, I have an advocate before the only one who can judge me, and my advocate is Jesus, the one who bears my judgment (1 John 2:1–2). I am not my relationships, but it is only through a personal relationship with Jesus Christ that I can come to the Father (John 14:6). It is so easy to get stuck in the distortions of identity. We have looked at only three distortions, yet we have exposed a paradigm for dismantling identity distortion and resetting gospel identity. It begins with realizing that no person, thing, or experience has the power to declare identity. However, we grant them this power when we harbor lies or distorted truths. When we realign ourselves to the truths of what God has said about his redeemed children, we have an identity that is impervious to lies and is crisis proof.

CHAPTER 4 ASSIGNMENT

Exposing Distortions

1) Read Acts 8:1–24. Considering Peter's description of Simon (vv. 20–23), what distortions were keeping him from experiencing the Holy Spirit?
2) Read Isaiah 6. What could allow you to accept a call like Isaiah's?
3) Read John 6. Why did people follow Jesus? Why did people quit following Jesus? Why did Peter keep following Jesus?
4) Read Mark 9:14–29. What role does faith have in relating to Jesus?
5) Read 1 Thessalonians 1:2–9. What were the Thessalonians known for? How had their identity changed?

Digging Deeper

As you study the life change of the people in the passages below, note how they moved from a distorted identity to a gospel identity.

Abraham (Genesis 12)
Isaac (Genesis 21)
Jacob (Genesis 25)
Joseph (Genesis 30)
Moses (Exodus 2)
Gideon (Judges 6)
Samson (Judges 13)
Ruth (Ruth)
Samuel (1 Samuel 1)
David (1 Samuel 16)
Hezekiah (2 Kings 18)
Josiah (2 Kings 22)
Jeremiah (Jeremiah 1)
Jonah (Jonah)
Job (Job 1; 39–42)
Nehemiah (Nehemiah 1)

Esther (Esther)
The paralytic (Mark 2)
Matthew (Matthew 9)
Peter (Matthew 4)
Thomas (John 20)
Zacchaeus (Luke 19)
Mary Magdalene (Luke 8; Matthew 28)
Nicodemus (John 3)
The Samaritan woman (John 4)
The criminal on the cross (Luke 23)
Paul (Acts 9)
Cornelius (Acts 10)

5

WORSHIP

A disciple is a worshiper—what mental picture comes to mind when you read that? The images people have shared with me range from an Old Testament priest slaughtering an atonement lamb, to a backwoods snake handler, to someone "slain in the Spirit" and rolling in the aisles. Worship often evokes a picture of a group gathered in religious oneness paying homage to their god through practices including singing, prayer, meditation, liturgy, and a word of encouragement from a spiritual leader.

While the preceding programming elements are part of the planning or evaluating of a worship service, they do not cause worship in which God is honored and praised or where worshipers humbly offer prayers of confession, gratitude, and dependence, as well as obedient service. The picture is framed wrong. Worship is not something we can program; it must be a grace-filled response to a divine encounter.

My family has lived mostly in the northwestern United States. We did however spend a few years living in the Midwest. One night, my boys were in the front yard and called me to come and see something. As I arrived on the scene, I found them enamored by fireflies. The boys decided to catch them in a jar. In the morning the boys (and I) were very disappointed to see that the dead bugs didn't glow. In the Northwest our bugs look pretty much the same dead or alive, but not so with a firefly—without its fire, it's pretty much an unremarkable gnat.

That experience often reminds me that God looks very different "captured" than he does free. When I try to capture God in a morning quiet time or in a weekly worship service, he often looks "fireless" to my observing soul. But when he's free or observed in life, discovered together with other worshipers and humbly asked to show up in a community group, I often find him awe-inspiring, fire-flickering, and life-giving.

Worship is responding to God for who he is, what he has done, and what he is doing. For an image bearer to worship, it means mirroring back to the Father, Son, and Holy Spirit who they are, in gratitude for what all three have done. When we reflect God's thinking, love what God loves, grieve over the things that grieve God, and mirror the mercy and comfort God has shown us, this is worship. Worship is as much about how we live un-gathered as it is the services in which we gather. "We do not go to church to worship. But as continuing worshipers, we gather ourselves together to continue our worship, but now in the company of brothers and sisters."[1]

As you work through this chapter on worshiping God, it is my hope and prayer that you do not merely acquire more data in your analysis of God, but that you become awestruck by his wonder, growing deeper in love with the Father, Son, and Holy Spirit.

The Father Seeks Worshipers

John's Gospel highlights the nature of worship in this interaction between a Samaritan woman and Jesus:

> The woman said to him, "Sir, I perceive that you are a prophet. Our fathers worshiped on this mountain, but you say that in Jerusalem is the place where people ought to worship." Jesus said to her, "Woman, believe me, the hour is coming when neither on this mountain nor in Jerusalem will you worship the Father. You worship what you do not know; we worship what we know, for salvation is from the Jews. But the hour is coming, and is now here, when the true worshipers will worship the

— what does that look like?

Father in spirit and truth, for the Father is seeking such people to worship him. God is spirit, and those who worship him must worship in spirit and truth." (John 4:19–24)

In the 1980s and 1990s the seeker-sensitive movement took hold of many churches. The premise of the movement is that unchurched people cannot understand the gospel message because it has become too "churchified," so it structures its services to accommodate the unchurched. The music, decor, format, and publications are all designed to build a bridge into the world of the unchurched and to remove barriers to the hearing of the gospel message.

Needless to say, some giant truths are overlooked for the sake of evangelism. First, the church is not defined as a service; it is the people of God, and as people of God we are to be worshipers of God. First Corinthians 14:24–25 indicates that when the presence of God is discernable among the people of God, it is a powerful evangelistic tool in the hands of God. Unbelieving people will fall down and worship, having been convinced of the realities of God and their own sinfulness. Second, when it comes to worship, God, not man, is the seeker (Rom. 3:10–12). A biblical seeker service, then, is one designed for God in which he would find his people worshiping in spirit and truth.

In John 4, we find a woman talking to Jesus about religious worship services on a Samaritan mountainside rather than in a Jewish temple in Jerusalem. Jesus was calling the woman to live her life as a worship service rather than calling her to go to one. "Jesus was saying that our meeting place with God would no longer be limited to physical structures, geographical locales, or specific times. . . . *Jesus* is where and how we meet with God."[2] Jesus was telling her that the Father is seeking those who will discover him "loose and on fire" in the everyday occurrences of life, responding to him in ways that please and glorify him.

Worship Is in Truth

I am constantly amazed by the truth that the Father is looking for those who will worship him in spirit and truth. My amazement quickly moves to a humble conviction, for it suggests that such worshipers are in short supply. There are worshipers who worship actual truth, and Jesus confronted such worshipers in his day: "You search the Scriptures because you think that in them you have eternal life; and it is they that bear witness about me, yet you refuse to come to me that you may have life" (John 5:39–40). Truth worshipers come in many forms:

- I am what I know, so the more I know about God or spiritual things, the godlier or more spiritual I will be.
- My truth system dictates the way things are and must be. God cannot move in ways outside my belief system.
- All things rationally reconcile.

I have a short list of biblical questions and a longer list of existential questions for which I have no satisfactory rational reconciliation. Other truth systems are riddled with rational conflicts as well, yet what I love about Christianity is not the nice and tidy axioms but the invitation to mystery, truth, and hope. The Bible is very real in telling us we are not wired to figure out life, God's work, or God himself. We are wired to learn, think, and bridge gaps with love and faith:

> Seek the LORD while he may be found;
>> call upon him while he is near;
> let the wicked forsake his way,
>> and the unrighteous man his thoughts;
> let him return to the LORD, that he may have compassion on him,
>> and to our God, for he will abundantly pardon.
> For my thoughts are not your thoughts,
>> neither are your ways my ways, declares the LORD.
> For as the heavens are higher than the earth,
>> so are my ways higher than your ways
>> and my thoughts than your thoughts. (Isa. 55:6–9)

If you are in the market for a truth system, don't be fooled by the "salesman" who tells you that questions about God can be completely bypassed by choosing a system without God. Everyone must deal with their worship wiring. For example, when thinking of the creation or origin of the universe, both God-centered and godless systems must deal with the same questions.

- Is anything eternal?
- How did life begin?
- How did the "order" of things happen?

For the creationist, the answer to each is, redundantly, "God." This is why the explanation of creation reflects unity within a God-centered worldview, why creationists see a "universe." If the answers are diversified—"Matter in some state or form is eternal"; "There was an epic but random life-producing burst of energy"; "Given enough time, anything has a chance of forming"—we simply end up farming out divine attributes such as eternality to matter, life-giving to chance, and design to time and chaos theories. In essence, both hearts worship, but one worships a recognizable nameable God, and the other worships truths, principles, or theories.

Truth worship is also exhibited when people worship the Bible rather than the God of the Bible. In its most subtle form, it appears this way: "I do what the Bible says," or "I obey the Bible." There is a sense in which this is true for all of Jesus's disciples. In an effort to reserve exaltation and glory for God, however, it may be helpful for us to remind one another that when we do what the Bible says, we are doing what God says, and we are obeying God. We want to read the Bible to know the God who gave us his revealed Word. Truth worshipers have developed what they think is a way to have right standing before the God of the Bible. They master the content of Scripture and religiously discipline themselves to adhere to its instruction.

Worship Is Spirit

"Spirit" is used to depict a number of things in Scripture. It is used for God's Spirit, the human spirit, spirit beings, and wind. There is a double meaning to be seen in the expression "worshiping in spirit." Paul recalibrates the Jewish sign of circumcision by pointing to internal heart expressions and away from exterior, outward expressions: "But a Jew is one inwardly, and circumcision is a matter of the heart, by the Spirit, not by the letter. His praise is not from man but from God" (Rom. 2:29). In this verse Paul takes the sign of the covenant and clarifies it, saying, "Here is the sign of the covenant, a heart that praises God by the Spirit of God." When the Father seeks worshipers, he seeks those who have had the dullness of their heart peeled away by the Spirit of God and made tender to the person and work of Jesus.

When Jesus talks to the woman at the well, he contrasts the worship of her people, the Samaritans, which appears to be in spirit (human spirit) and without truth or understanding, with the worship of his people, which appears to be in truth (according to the traditions and writings of Moses) without spirit. It is easy to run to polarized options in worship services: spirit, meaning "participatory and engaged," and truth, meaning "accurate and/ or provocative."

Think about what Jesus was saying to this woman. She had come to the well in the heat of the day rather than in the cool of the morning, which would have been a more traditional time for women to come to the well. She came alone, and Jesus brought up the fact that she has had five husbands and now has a live-in boyfriend. These are not good credentials on a social register. He was telling a woman who may well have been a social outcast that the Father God was seeking people to worship him in spirit and truth, but he was not finding this worship in either the Samaritan or Jewish culture.

Worship is not to be a cultural expression but a personal expression, transforming the human spirit through mysterious uniting with the Holy Spirit in oneness. Yet this Holy Spirit is not a force; he is a person of the Godhead, and as such, he desires for the other two persons to be worshiped as well. He therefore guides in truth. Concerning the Holy Spirit's ministry in the lives of his disciples, Jesus said:

> Nevertheless, I tell you the truth: it is to your advantage that I go away, for if I do not go away, the Helper will not come to you. But if I go, I will send him to you. And when he comes, he will convict the world concerning sin and righteousness and judgment: concerning sin, because they do not believe in me; concerning righteousness, because I go to the Father, and you will see me no longer; concerning judgment, because the ruler of this world is judged. I still have many things to say to you, but you cannot bear them now. When the Spirit of truth comes, he will guide you into all the truth, for he will not speak on his own authority, but whatever he hears he will speak, and he will declare to you the things that are to come. He will glorify me, for he will take what is mine and declare it to you. All that the Father has is mine; therefore I said that he will take what is mine and declare it to you. (John 16:7–15)

The Holy Spirit convicts, guides into all truth, speaks what he hears from Jesus, and glorifies Jesus. Jesus says that since the Father is one with him, this means that the Holy Spirit points to the things of the Father as well. David Peterson differentiates between the human spirit and the Holy Spirit, pointing to the latter as the primary reference in John 4: "The Holy Spirit, who regenerates us, brings new life, and confirms us in the truth."[3] To worship in spirit, then, means that our spirit is definitely engaged with the working of the Holy Spirit. To worship in spirit also means a life dominated or controlled by the Spirit. Look at these words from the apostle Paul:

> Therefore do not be foolish, but understand what the will of the Lord is. And do not get drunk with wine, for that is debauchery, but be filled with the Spirit, addressing one another in psalms

and hymns and spiritual songs, singing and making melody to the
Lord with your heart, giving thanks always and for everything to
God the Father in the name of our Lord Jesus Christ, submitting
to one another out of reverence for Christ. (Eph. 5:17–21)

Paul is describing someone filled with the Spirit, yet he goes
on to illustrate this Spirit-filling in the everyday relationships of
husband/wife, master/slave, and parent/child. Paul had in mind
worshipers, filled by the Holy Spirit, who speak to one another in
psalms, hymns, and spiritual songs, having an internal melody
playing in their heart along with continuous thanks and respect
for others. This doesn't sound like a service on a Samaritan
mountain or in a Jerusalem temple; this sounds like living as a
worshiper in spirit and filled with the Spirit of truth.

Worship Is Love

As we have seen, Jesus believed that the greatest command is to
love God with our whole being. Jonathan Edwards describes the
redeemed heart's posture toward God as "religious affections."
About God, John Piper says, "He is most glorified when I am
most satisfied in him."[4] The apostle John writes:

Beloved, let us love one another, for love is from God, and whoever loves has been born of God and knows God. Anyone who
does not love does not know God, because God is love. In this
the love of God was made manifest among us, that God sent
his only Son into the world, so that we might live through him.
In this is love, not that we have loved God but that he loved us
and sent his Son to be the propitiation for our sins. Beloved, if
God so loved us, we also ought to love one another. No one has
ever seen God; if we love one another, God abides in us and his
love is perfected in us. (1 John 4:7–12)

In a culture marinated in romance novels and chick flicks,
biblical love may be a hard concept to grasp. Love is more than
emotions. God describes himself as a scorned lover, a jealous

God, a covenant-keeping and faithful God, and a Father, and Jesus is described as our brother. God uses many descriptions to portray his people: children, body, bride, and sheep. The challenge is tying these portraits of God and his people together. We are his children, and Jesus invites us to pray, "Our Father." We are the body of Christ. We are the bride, and Jesus is the bridegroom. We are sheep, and Jesus is the good shepherd. Each of these metaphors is chosen to call us into meaningful relationship with God. It is impossible to worship the Father, the Son, and the Holy Spirit without loving them. Look at Jesus's prayer for those who would believe in him because of his disciples:

> I do not ask for these only, but also for those who will believe in me through their word, that they may all be one, just as you, Father, are in me, and I in you, that they also may be in us, so that the world may believe that you have sent me. The glory that you have given me I have given to them, that they may be one even as we are one, I in them and you in me, that they may become perfectly one, so that the world may know that you sent me and loved them even as you loved me. Father, I desire that they also, whom you have given me, may be with me where I am, to see my glory that you have given me because you loved me before the foundation of the world. O righteous Father, even though the world does not know you, I know you, and these know that you have sent me. I made known to them your name, and I will continue to make it known, that the love with which you have loved me may be in them, and I in them. (John 17:20–26)

Can you see the love between Jesus and the Father? Do you see his repeated use of the word "one"?

> *The triune plan of salvation, the* pactum salutis, *flows from, through and to the Father's eternal love for the Son in the Spirit.* The triune God has eternally desired to bless his people with the greatest possible gift and the greatest possible gift he can give is nothing other than the enjoyment of his own eternal,

fecund fellowship. Communion in the Son's eternal life of love, glory and giving with the Father in the Spirit constitutes the ultimate blessing of the gospel.[5]

He describes himself and the Father as one, his desire for believers to be one, and his desire for believers to experience the oneness that Jesus and the Father share. The Bible describes two people coming together in marriage as becoming one. The picture is love. Worship is our being one with the object of our worship.

The apostle Paul warns the Corinthians of the gross sin of uniting their bodies with the bodies of prostitutes: "Do you not know that your bodies are members of Christ? Shall I then take the members of Christ and make them members of a prostitute? Never! Or do you not know that he who is joined to a prostitute becomes one body with her? For, as it is written, 'The two will become one flesh.' But he who is joined to the Lord becomes one spirit with him" (1 Cor. 6:15–17). Paul, in graphic language and illustration, is portraying the intimate nature of being one with Jesus. Worship is not casual. It is not a one-hour "quickie" on Sunday morning, but it is a life lived at one with another life. This relationship is a part of what the Bible describes as love.

Worship Is Glory

Just as Jesus describes the Holy Spirit as one who will glorify him and, in turn, the Father, since Jesus glorifies the Father (John 17:1, 26), so our worship is about glorifying God: Father, Son, and Holy Spirit. There are two words in particular that help shape a view of glorifying God. The first is the Hebrew word *kabod*. Within this word's meanings is the idea of weight. In English we speak of "the weight of glory," and we refer to someone with influence and power as a "heavy hitter."

> This expression simply refers to his manifest presence. If, in some contexts, this is associated with phenomena such as clouds and lightning and fire, it is not to be thought that God

somehow identified with these things. They serve only to conceal the true power, majesty and magnificence of God, which would destroy anyone to whom he might reveal himself fully.[6]

First Samuel 4 tells the story of Israel's bringing the ark of the covenant to battle against the Philistines. Israel is defeated, and the ark is captured by the Philistines. When news of this reaches Eli's daughter-in-law, she is in the throes of childbirth. She is so distressed over her husband's death, the defeat of Israel, and the capture of the ark that she names her son Ichabod, which means "the glory has departed." *Kabod* is part of this boy's name, but rather than his being named "glory bearer" or "imager," he is named under the cloud of the glory of God departing from his family and nation.

The glory of God is not measurable by laboratory protocol, but the Bible is clear that the glory of God is something that people are to be aware of, to experience, and to express. The epic moments of provision and punishment in the Old Testament narratives can so capture our imagination that we forget that God was, in the process, instilling the nature of his presence in his people. It was the everyday fingerprints of God that were to grab their attention and lead them to worship:

- Trees, mountains, and hills: "You shall go out in joy and be led forth in peace; the mountains and the hills before you shall break forth into singing, and all the trees of the field shall clap their hands" (Isa. 55:12).
- Animals: The voice of the LORD makes the deer give birth and strips the forests bare, and in his temple all cry, 'Glory!'" (Ps. 29:9).
- Heavens: "Praise him, sun and moon, praise him, all you shining stars!" (Ps. 148:3).

The very weight of life giving is to be awe inspiring. This weighty glory resident within the people of Israel was to be their distinction. *Holy* means "set apart." The people of God are set apart by the weight of God's glory for the purpose of others beholding him and in turn responding to him. Given this great responsibility, the Israelites gravitated toward pride, assuming that God had entrusted his glory to them because of their own merit, when in fact it was because of God's grace.

They also thought that if they could insulate the glory or holiness of God from the common or profane things of their world that they could keep their special standing as glory bearers. However, God intends for his glory to be a heavy distinction in the lives of his people. He wants his glory to be the overarching factor in decisions, relationships, and lifestyle, not for the sake of *protecting* the glory of God but rather for *displaying* the glory of God.

It is interesting that each of the items listed above became an idol in Israel. Trees were idolized (Jer. 2:26–27), and mountains were made into high places (Ezek. 6:13). Animals were made into sacred images as well as sun, moon, and stars (2 Kings 17:16). God inspired worship literature to call his people into using his creation as a catalyst for beholding his glory and joining in it as image bearers. This still holds true today. God's creation is a choir declaring his glory. Yet people are his crowning creation for just such an assignment as declaring the glory of God.

The second word for *glory* is the Greek word *doxa*. This word contains the idea of light or brilliance as well as of excellence. This word *doxa* is used today to describe a championship team as well as a high-end designer watch.[7] When the word is used of God in relationship to his people, it means that we are to declare his excellencies. We cannot add anything to God; again, it is imaging who he is and what he has done, pointing back to Jesus as the champion and to our salvation as God's excellent work in process. To live a life of *doxa* is to live displaying the good works God has prepared for us. It is, as Paul prays, to walk worthy of our calling: "From the day we heard, we have not ceased to pray for you, asking that you may be filled with the knowledge of his will in all spiritual wisdom and understanding, so as to walk in a manner worthy of the Lord, fully pleasing to him, bearing fruit in every good work and increasing in the knowledge of God" (Col. 1:9–10).

Most discussion regarding worship has to do with who or what gets exalted—Jesus, feelings, the worshiper. If we worship in spirit, truth, and love, we lean in the opposite direction of idolatry. Paul described the 180-degree experience of the Thessalonians this way: "You turned to God from idols to serve the living and true God" (1 Thess. 1:9). Jesus said that a person cannot serve two masters (Matt. 6:24), and this service includes worship. You cannot worship the living and true God while serving idols. The minute you try to manage God, juggling him with anything else as a priority, you have ceased to recognize his weightiness (*kabod*) and his excellence (*doxa*).

God has designed his people to shine light on the world, not as the sun but as a moon reflecting the very light of the sun. We are called to reflect the light of Jesus. David Peterson writes, "Man, then, was created in God's image so that he or she might represent God, like an ambassador from a foreign country."[8] John the apostle distinguished John the Baptist as a proclaimer of Jesus from Jesus the proclaimed: "There was a man sent from God, whose name was John. He came as a witness, to bear witness about the light, that all might believe through him. He was not the light, but came to bear witness about the light" (John 1:6–8). There is as much to learn about worship in the apostle's words as there is to learn about mission. John the Baptist was sent to bear witness about the light; he was not the light, but his witness was a catalyst for belief. Those who worship in spirit, truth, and love inspire worship of the same kind. When we align ourselves to the true and living God in oneness, this is worship. When it is observed, it is a convincing apologetic of Jesus's claims.

I hope your thinking about worship has been challenged. Perhaps you now see that worship goes far beyond what happens in an organized religious service, but that it has everything to do with heart and soul and life and passion and truth.

CHAPTER 5 ASSIGNMENT

Exposing Yourself to the Nature of Worship

1) Read Psalms 27, 73, and 84, and record your observations about worship.
2) Read Exodus 20:1–11. What is the correspondence between obedience and worship?
3) Read Psalm 103. What do you think it means to "bless the LORD"?
4) Read Isaiah 40 and record the awe-inspiring aspects of God.
5) Read 1 John 4:7–21. What do you observe about God's love? How does it enhance your worship?

Digging Deeper

In this chapter we have said repeatedly that to worship is to respond to God for who he is and for what he has done. Use the truths about him that are listed below as a springboard to responding to him in worship.

Incommunicable Attributes (those that are unique to God):
Independence (Acts 17:24–25)
Unchangeableness (immutability) (Ps. 102:25–27)
Eternity (Ps. 90:2)
Omnipresence (Ps. 139:7–10)
Unity (simplicity) (Ex. 34:6–7)
Immensity (1 Kings 8:27)

Communicable Attributes (those that are operated upon us or the world):
Spirituality (John 4:24)
Invisibility (1 Tim. 1:17)
Knowledge (omniscience) (1 John 3:20)
Wisdom (Rom. 16:27)
Truthfulness (Jer. 10:10–11)
Faithfulness (Num. 23:19)

Goodness (Luke 18:19)
Love (1 John 4:8)
Compassion (Matt. 9:6)
Mercy (2 Sam. 24:14)
Grace (Rom. 9:15)
Patience (Ex. 34:6)
Holiness (Isa. 6:3)
Peace/Order (1 Cor. 14:33)
Righteousness (Deut. 32:4)
Jealousy (Isa. 48:11)
Wrath (Rom. 1:18)
Will (Eph. 1:11)
Freedom (Ps. 115:3)
Omnipotence (power) (Matt. 19:26)
Perfection (Matt. 5:48)
Blessedness (happiness) (1 Tim. 6:15)
Beauty (Ps. 73:25)
Glory (Ps. 24:10)

6

WORSHIP DISTORTIONS

I was asked to teach an intensive course at a seminary, three eight-hour days of presentation. During the first hour my agenda was to introduce the idea that we are all idolaters. I began by saying, "One hundred percent of your pastoral counseling will involve identifying and confronting idols." Immediately the push back began: "Idolatry is a primitive idea"; "People don't have idols; they have issues." As long as we ignore what the Bible says about the human heart and what God desires from his people, we will raise these same objections. The Bible says, "The heart is deceitful above all things, and desperately sick; who can understand it?" (Jer. 17:9).

The root of idolatry is pride. Isaiah described Lucifer's rebellion as he ceased to worship because he wanted to be worshiped: "You said in your heart, 'I will ascend to heaven; above the stars of God I will set my throne on high; I will sit on the mount of assembly in the far reaches of the north; I will ascend above the heights of the clouds; I will make myself like the Most High.'" (Isa. 14:13–14). Isaiah prophesies of the coming day of the Lord and how God will have ultimate triumph over all his enemies and all rebellious movements. Isaiah describes pride and idolatry as being ultimately destroyed when God completes the establishment of his kingdom.[1]

Again, in James, pride is seen as a heart condition that God resists. The posture appropriate to approaching God is one of humility:

Or do you suppose it is to no purpose that the Scripture says, "He yearns jealously over the spirit that he has made to dwell in us"? But he gives more grace. Therefore it says, "God opposes the proud, but gives grace to the humble." Submit yourselves therefore to God. Resist the devil, and he will flee from you. . . . Humble yourselves before the Lord, and he will exalt you. (James 4:5–7, 10)

Pride is seen as detestable to God precisely because it steals from God's glory and his preeminence. Pride is rebellion, but it is much more than rebellion against God's authority. Pride is self-centeredness rather than God-centeredness. A proud heart sees itself as central and God as the one who must find his place of orbit in the proud heart's universe. While few people who call themselves Christians would admit to such a self-centered worldview, I find my weeks filled with people with questions and comments such as these:

- How can God be loving and let this bad thing happen to me?
- I can't believe in a God who lets bad things happen.
- I don't care what the Bible says; this is what I want.
- I have been praying for a Christian husband, and if God wanted me to marry one, then he would have provided one.
- If God is against homosexuality, why did he create me this way?
- If God wanted me to stay married, he should have told that to my cheating spouse.

Look beyond the content of those objections to the underlying conviction of those who are making them. The objectors believe they have rights and God has the responsibility to work within those rights. To their way of thinking, God can't love and also do something the objector can't understand, nor can God call for behavior that is inconvenient or politically incorrect. They believe that God has no right to ask them to opt for grace and forgive another when they have a "biblical" right to hurt someone who has hurt them.

A couple of things need to be pointed out. First, the idea that God is accountable to us for his behavior, or at least for explanations for acting as he does, skews our real place with God. At best, it makes him our peer, and in that vein he should give us a reasonable explanation. I have friends and relatives who are engineers and scientists, and they often take the fun out of the mystery in things such as fireworks, ocean waves, and roller coasters. Their explanations go into areas that I am neither interested in nor capable of understanding. However, I would hope that an infinitely wise God has a rationale that is far above my understanding. When I talk to people who are angry at God for what he has done or is allowing to happen, I often hear them say, "All I want to know is why." I have asked several of them, "Really? What if his explanation didn't satisfy you, and you were convinced he could achieve the same end without doing or allowing what has angered you?" At that point, they often realize that they really want more than a why; they want a why that satisfies them and that makes God accountable to them.

Second, the concept of creature and creator gives God a trump card. He really does get to design his world, his creations, and his story for his own glory. Anything that attempts to compete with that is an idol. Pride paints us into a corner between self-centeredness and idolatry. Very few people are impressed or enamored with self-absorption; it seems like it should be so easy to detect as well as build a firewall to keep oneself from lapsing into it. The problem is that pride is subtle to its host even though it appears brazen to the audience. Next, we'll look at three gateways through which pride enters the heart.

Gateways for Pride

Pleasure

Legion are the number of assaults mounted upon us from media and advertising. The sloganeering of America has left us believing there is a "my way" to fast-food preparation, a percentage of an insurance premium that just fifteen minutes of time will save me, and that cosmetic companies design products because "you are worth it." Do a quick assessment: do you find the common denominator in the marketing strategy? Surprise! It is you. You are led to believe that products and companies orbit around your rights, comforts, and desires. The bombardment of such subtle messages of self-centeredness takes a toll, and we start to believe that our pleasure is not an indulgence but an entitlement. Thoughts start to cascade: "I should have a car, house, clothes, food, spouse, and faith that please me." Once my pleasure becomes the value giver, I am free to use them and consume them as commodities. If they fail to deliver self-gratifying experiences, I can replace, abandon, disown, or discredit them. Even if I am exposed to something as value-free as coffee, I am challenged to brand loyalty through other values such as fair trade, ecology, or punch-card discounts. It all boils down to what satisfies or gratifies me most. Do I want to help, save, or enjoy? Does one of my desires trump the others, or does the company with the best alchemy of values win my patronage?

In the mix of companies catering to my desires and enticing me to acquire their product, my heart becomes shaped to view life from this consumerist vantage point. God becomes one more marketer after my worship equity. If as a gatekeeper I do not keep pleasure and desire contained, I will soon find myself adrift in the options market of idolatry. If I don't like the seeming harshness of God's sovereignty, I can shape a god who knowingly responds to my predispositions. If I want a god who can roll with the punches, I can be more open about the future and human decisions. If I want a god who is friendlier to historically marginalized groups such as women and gays, I can develop a trajectory hermeneutic that allows me to maximize the rights of such groups by marginalizing the timelessness of the Scriptures. Forgive the little rant, but what often gets promoted as progressive, enlightened, or culturally liberated is most always a new attempt at an old ploy, i.e., reshaping God into my image.

This becomes a form of pride, as it refuses to submit and surrender to God as master and prefers to recast God's role in the story to that of servant. I talk with people almost daily who are shocked and whose world is rocked because God is not pleasing them, and to them his performance is inexcusable. Paul asks a question of his readers: "But who are you, O man, to answer back to God? Will what is molded say to its molder, 'Why have you made me like this?' Has the potter no right over the clay, to make out of the same lump one vessel for honorable use and another for dishonorable use?" (Rom. 9:20–21).

How different would your thought process be if you saw God at the center and that all things and people are designed to please God? I find myself prone to "worship drift." I am in constant need of worship realignment, to recalibrate from my sensual, consumerist pleasure center to find my meaning and fulfillment in pleasing God.

Power

We are also inclined to express our pride through the area of control. Interestingly enough, we often look at those who take charge, who persevere and change a system or a structure, as leaders. Their stories and accomplishments are meant to inspire us. *Beyond the Glory* is a documentary series of sport celebrities that takes a look behind the competitive accomplishments and discloses pain, brokenness, and relational tragedy. The seemingly endless supply of such stories indicates a phenomenon that has occurred in our image-driven culture: we have substituted *celebrity* for *hero*. Heroes act heroically, regardless of the fame it brings; celebrities stand out for their accomplishments, regardless of their character. Celebrities are often willing to take shortcuts through steroids, embezzlement, or a myriad of coping medications just for the opportunity to be at the top.

Idolatry creeps in when our desire for the spotlight emboldens us to walk in darkness. Pride as power justifies its actions as a means to an end. Power subtly vies for our sense of identity. We no longer find ourselves needing to trust God, or perhaps we fear that God will not provide for us as we desire, so we take matters into our own hands.

Some years ago, I met with a man who wanted to get married. He was all for praying that God would provide a wife. As time went on, the young man began to feel that God needed some help in introducing him to a marriage partner. He finally did meet a woman to whom he was attracted, quickly and profoundly. They both did a great job of putting their best foot forward, and within a few short months they were married. Another few months went by, and the young man wanted to see me again, this time because he had made a mistake, he said, and he wanted help on how to get out of the marriage. When I told him that God desires redemption to come out of his marriage, that marriage is one of God's tools for transforming lives, he wanted none of it. He had heard advice to slow down the relationship before the marriage, and he had ignored it, and he continued to demonstrate his skill at ignoring advice at the speed of darkness.

He is an example of someone who believes in the principles of God, yet when it comes to the cost of discipleship is unwilling to surrender his will to God. To this day, this man is still seeking to control the course of his own life. He takes God's Word and will under advisement, but ultimately his decisions are based on what he wants to do. He tries to be in charge of his life, and as a result, he doesn't know God as Lord or as a powerful God who can work in the midst of unforeseen and unpleasant circumstances. To him, God is more like a tool in the profile of personal wealth management: if he functions like a well-performing stock or commodity, then use him, but if he isn't getting you where you want to be, then trade him, sell him, or ignore him. Such a person is often found in the double bind of assessing personal value and progress by big achievements, while living at relative smallness in his relationships.

Several years ago, I was directing one of the largest university ministries in the country; it was in Washington State, which at the time competed with Oregon for being the least churched state in America. I was also on the advisory board for an international ministry that eventually asked me to serve as their North American director of student ministries. I accepted the invitation and within the year transitioned to the main office. My new position had me flying back and forth across the country giving seminars, writing articles, and speaking at national youth events. During the last year I worked with this ministry, I was on the road for 180 days, and I began to experience some identity drift. I was what I did, and I was my speaking gigs.

Power measures meaning by how many things you have going, by the number of people who report to you, by popularity, or by how many follow your tweets. God measures meaning by a humble heart willing to achieve or to leave the biggest deal on the table for the love of Jesus. Anything else is an idol. Pride subtly replaces your identity as an image bearer with an identity of your own creating. Power demands tremendous sacrifice, but the sacrifice is not a joyful response to the work of Christ. Eventually it becomes a resented payment, just like when someone sells his house at a loss but has to continue to make payments on it. Power overpromises freedom and under-delivers with bondage.

People

A third way we express pride is through our relationships. Pride comes into play in the place or priority that people hold in our lives. An unguarded heart will allow "the fear of man" to become a dominant posture. Jesus warns against this in the challenges he gives: "I tell you, my friends, do not fear those who kill the body, and after that have nothing more that they can do. But I will warn you whom to fear: fear him who, after he has killed, has authority to cast into hell. Yes, I tell you, fear him!" (Luke 12:4–5). Jesus is telling his listeners that they are more concerned about people who can punish them in the short term than one who can punish them forever. In short, we get sideways when we avoid pain and pursue approval at the expense of revering God as ultimate. When God becomes a commodity placed in cold storage so that we might enjoy the seasonal fruit of self-promotion or protection, we have found a new audience for reverential fear or worship, which smacks of idolatry at its finest. Notice how Jesus responds to challenges:

> They came again to Jerusalem. And as he was walking in the temple, the chief priests and the scribes and the elders came to him, and they said to him, "By what authority are you doing these things, or who gave you this authority to do them?" Jesus said to them, "I will ask you one question; answer me, and I will tell you by what authority I do these things. Was the baptism of John from heaven or from man? Answer me." And they discussed it with one another, saying, "If we say, 'From heaven,' he will say, 'Why then did you not believe him?' But shall we say, 'From man'?"— they were afraid of the people, for they all held that John really was a prophet. So they answered Jesus, "We do not know." And Jesus said to them, "Neither will I tell you by what authority I do these things." (Mark 11:27–33)

Here, we see religious power brokers confronting Jesus for practicing religion without a license. With his authority challenged, rather than bowing down to his inquisitors, he asks a question that reveals their own fear-of-man issues. He tells them that he will talk to them about his authority source if they will identify what they believed to be John the Baptist's authority source. Paralyzed between their lack of respect for John's message and their inordinate craving for the respect of the people, they cannot commit to answering Jesus. Their paralysis allows Jesus to walk away from them free from the fear of man, living out the fear of God.

I hope that passage shows you just how the fear of man is related to idolatry. Those religious leaders, trapped between fear-of-man traditions and approval ratings, were not free to recognize the spiritual reality of John's ministry, nor were they able to embrace Jesus as the Christ. Similarly, when people keep us from responding freely to God, we find ourselves in the idolatrous territory of making people ultimate and giving them the authority to dictate the terms for relating to God. This proverb serves as a great warning: "The fear of man lays a snare, but whoever trusts in the LORD is safe" (Prov. 29:25).

Such a proverb makes me ask what's so safe about not fearing man? I suspect the answer is deeper than "Because God is always the right pick." I think the answer goes to the very core of who we are and who God is. As people, we have limits, and we are dependent on all kinds of circumstances and conditions. God, on the other hand, has no limits and is free to move within the conditions of his own making. From a pragmatic standpoint, then, people who order their life for the approval of man put themselves in double jeopardy. First, they have no idea if they will actually get the approval they seek, and, second, it is likely that the approval will be short-lived.

Conversely, those who seek God's approval know that:

- Jesus is the gateway to acceptance (1 Pet. 2:5).
- Jesus is the way to the Father (John 14:6).
- Reconciliation is provided through Jesus (Rom. 5:11).
- God never changes (Mal. 3:6).
- Every good gift comes from God (James 1:17).

When you consider how unsure and unstable are the praise and approval of man, it is baffling that worshiping God is so quickly abandoned for such faint applause.

Even Christian culture can become an environment for practicing idolatry. We create a subculture of comfortable and pleasure-filled lives. We develop story lines for why we should be blessed for living differently from the world that rebels against its Creator. Yet this subculture is shaped not so much by the kingdom and the values of God as it is by a stained-glass version of the flesh. Jesus already raised the bar from adultery to a heart of lust and from murder of a brother to anger. So how is it we continue to smuggle sin and knock-off versions of righteousness into lives and community in the name of Christianity? It has to have something to do with who or what we are worshiping. When self is at the center, things that feel good or right, emotional places of consolation or insulation, or distractions and attractions don't seem that bad. But when God is the center, when the God of the universe comes into your soul, living quarters become tight, and there just isn't any room for things that don't exalt the Father, the Son, and the Holy Spirit. Let's evaluate this from two different perspectives.

Perspective 1: What Makes Me Angry

Many of you have learned to live with a manageable amount of anger. It may play out in traffic (road rage). It may play out in complaining or controlling behavior. Coaches step down weekly during little league and soccer seasons, and it is not because of the kids. It's because of parents who are upset that their kid hasn't been given enough playing or development time or encouragement. When you can identify a source of anger, you are very close to identifying an idol. Parents who get their meaning and identity from their children and their children's achievements have created a deity from their child. People who get angry because of unexpected expenses may identify their shrine in their bank account.

We can observe Jesus's anger at the temple (Mark 11:15–19). It does not appear that Jesus had an agenda other than to keep the temple a place of reverence and prayer, but it had become a place of merchandising and profiteering. Jesus was angered, and his anger directs us to his God. James tells us that the anger of man does not produce the righteousness of God (James 1:20), but a man's anger certainly helps us identify what he deifies.

Perspective 2: What Frightens Me

Do you find yourself saying, "That scared me!" at least once a day? If you don't, I'm guessing that you know someone who uses that phrase a lot. And if you live a fairly fearless life, you are probably a regular source of *scary* for someone who is easily frightened. What makes us afraid can serve as a great trail of bread crumbs to lead us to where our idols live. We often build idols of the heart around the very things that give us a sense of security or make us feel safe. The inventory can be large and diverse, including careers and employment, assets such as savings and property, and relationships with friends and family.

A litmus test for parents to test whether their children have become idols is their response when one of the children gets deathly sick. Do they make attractive offers in an effort to entice God to heal: "If you'll heal my daughter, I'll go to church, give money, and quit smoking." God doesn't barter with us for our devotion, and he doesn't negotiate his grace. Rather, our devotion is brought about by his grace in our lives. We have nothing with which to barter. "The worship of the living and true God is essentially an engagement with him on the terms that he proposes and in the way that he alone makes possible."[2] Yet our anxiousness, our fear, and the panic that comes from imagining the worst-case scenario can be telltale indicators that we are distorting God or erecting a whole new one in his place. Here are a few verses regarding the peace that is found in the heart of a worshiper:

> You keep him in perfect peace whose mind is stayed on you,
>   because he trusts in you. (Isa. 26:3)

> Do not be anxious about anything, but in everything by prayer and supplication with thanksgiving let your requests be made known to God. And the peace of God, which surpasses all un-

derstanding, will guard your hearts and your minds in Christ Jesus. (Phil. 4:6–7)

For God gave us a spirit not of fear but of power and love and self-control. (2 Tim. 1:7)

Fear abducts us from the worshipful presence of God, making ransom demands for our release. The good news is that we have already been ransomed: "For there is one God, and there is one mediator between God and men, the man Christ Jesus, who gave himself as a ransom for all" (1 Tim. 2:5–6). To live afraid of loss is to completely misunderstand the nature of God's kingdom. Jesus contrasts his purpose with those of Satan: "The thief comes only to steal and kill and destroy. I came that they may have life and have it abundantly" (John 10:10).

The kingdom of God is an economy of abundance, while the economy of Satan is one of scarcity. When we live in fear of loss and are compelled to hoard blessings, we reveal our too-small view of God. Hopefully we can see the distortion that believes, "God isn't really going to provide for me," or, "If I want this, I have to take it." We must repent of this view of God that sees him on budgetary restraints or as one who miserly dispenses blessings. A view of God and life that fears placing ourselves completely in his hand and having only what he would desire is a distortion of a good and loving God. This view of God will prohibit worshiping God; it will cause us to drift to longing for provisions and being more excited about God's blessing than about God himself.

Can you see how idolatry seeps through the cracks of counterfeit Christianities such as moralism, religion, and prosperity? It is critical that, as followers of Christ, he is our only foundation (1 Cor. 3:10–15). We have the opportunity to live life from an eternal perspective. I believe that there is more continuity than discontinuity between the life Jesus lived on earth and the life he now lives in heaven. "Jesus is our starting point for all true knowledge, and therefore for theology. He is the goal toward which we move. We see this in our Christian existence, for we begin life as God's children when we are united to Christ by faith in his saving work, and our destiny is to be finally made like his image."[3] But contrary to this saving work of Christ, we have idolized even death and heaven, making them our functional saviors. We give ourselves permission to live lesser lives since we are not yet completed and sin still exists, but this is exactly the hothouse environment in which idols grow. They flourish in the soil of anger and fear. They grow strong in the heat of selfish desires and ambitions. They bloom in the light, being thought of as essential for our very happiness and survival.

I love the popular emphasis on dismantling the distinction between the sacred and the secular, but in an effort to make everything sacred, we have forgotten scriptural warnings against profaning God. When we distort God into our own image we profane his name and his glory:

> For my name's sake I defer my anger,
> > for the sake of my praise I restrain it for you,
> > that I may not cut you off.
> Behold, I have refined you, but not as silver;
> > I have tried you in the furnace of affliction.
> For my own sake, for my own sake, I do it,
> > for how should my name be profaned?
> > My glory I will not give to another. (Isa. 48:9–11)

But the children rebelled against me. They did not walk in my statutes and were not careful to obey my rules, by which, if a person does them, he shall live; they profaned my Sabbaths. Then I said I would pour out my wrath upon them and spend my anger against them in the wilderness. But I withheld my hand and acted for the sake of my name, that it should not be profaned in the sight of the nations, in whose sight I had brought them out. Moreover, I swore to them in the wilderness that I would scatter them among the nations and disperse them through the countries, because they had not obeyed my rules, but had rejected my statutes and profaned my Sabbaths, and their eyes were set on their fathers' idols. (Ezek. 20:21–24)

In just these couple of charges brought against his people, God through his prophets identifies disobedience, rebellion, and idolatry as means of profaning him. We must be careful to understand the gift that has been given to humans. We have been called to image the holy Creator of the universe. To live life as common, to reflect life as mere biology, economics, or social science, is to profane the mystery of life. When Jesus said that he is life, he was claiming deity; he was declaring life through him to be sacred; he was inviting us to life as worshipers. To live life without Jesus as center is to live life as an idolater.

CHAPTER 6 ASSIGNMENT

Read the narrative of the golden calf (Exodus 32). Take time to journal and reflect on these biblical passages on idolatry.

Exposing Yourself to the Biblical Concept of Idolatry

1) Read Genesis 11:1–9. What was the motive for building the Tower of Babel? What was God's evaluation of the project?
2) Read 1 Samuel 13:8–15. How does Saul reflect a heart of religious idolatry?
3) Read Luke 16:19–37. What idols do you think Jesus was confronting by telling his story?
4) Read Luke 19:1–10. What did it look like for Zacchaeus to be delivered from idolatrous priorities?
5) Read Acts 17:16–34. How did Paul use the Greeks' idols to present the gospel?

Digging Deeper

Observe from the passages below attitudes, behaviors, and consequences of worshiping something other than God. Make note of ways in which you sense a vulnerability to idolatry.

Old Testament
Psalm 115:4–8
Psalm 135:15–18
Deuteronomy 4:27–28
1 Kings 12:28–33
Psalm 106:19–21
Jeremiah 2:5–24
Jeremiah 5:7–19
Jeremiah 7:9–31
Jeremiah 11:8–13
Jeremiah 25:4–6
Jeremiah 35:15
Jeremiah 44:3–19

Ezekiel 40:4; 44:7–13
Ezekiel 11:18–21; 12:2
Hosea 4:16–17; 8:4–7; 10:5, 11; 13:2–3

New Testament
Matthew 15:1–20
Mark 7:6–13
John 12:35–46
Acts 7:46–52
Acts 17:24–25; 19:24–26
Acts 28:25–28
Romans 1:18–28
1 Corinthians 10:14–22
Revelation 9:17–21
Revelation 13:11–17

7

ping pong chapter

COMMUNITY

God's story has many dramatic scenes filled with heroic men of faith. Abraham obeyed God's call and comes out of an idolatrous pantheon to worship the one true God. Joseph survived incredible mistreatment and rose to second in command of the world-dominating Egypt. Moses led Israel with many signs and wonders through an epic exodus experience. King David reigned over Israel, enlarging her borders. In our Western world, dominated by self-actualization, it's hard to move beyond the desire to be the heroes of our own faith to see God's desire that his people be immersed in a community of faith. "God made us as persons-in-community to be the vehicle through which he would reveal his glory. . . . Jesus came to create a people who would model what it means to live under his rule."[1] Let's revisit these heroes of the faith and see how God used them to shape the people of his story.

Abraham is graced with the faith to believe God's covenant promises, that through his lineage the world would be blessed. Joseph was able to see the providential hand of God in his hardships, which resulted in Israel's surviving a famine and residing in Egypt. Moses, educated in the house of Pharaoh, was inspired by God to frame the moral, civil, and ceremonial codes that distinguished Israel as the people of God. David was inspired by God to model and resource Israel and, later, the church with heartfelt worship through the Psalms.

Fast-forward centuries to the book of Acts, where we find two sermons with different effects. The first is in Acts 2, where Peter preached on the day of Pentecost, and over three thousand people responded to the gospel message of Jesus. The second is in Acts 7, where Stephen preached, and his audience was enraged and stoned him to death. Both men were faithful to their God. One was catalytic in jump-starting the church, and the other ignited a persecution that was instrumental in causing the church to scatter and take the gospel beyond the borders of comfort.

God continues to move his people through the lives of individuals throughout the centuries of church history. Calvin's amazing *Institutes* come alive in the context of God's using him as an instrument for reforming his church. Martin Luther's zeal was based in his desire to see people worshiping in spirit and truth. Jonathan Edwards, considered by some to be the greatest theologian born in North America, chose a "lesser" post as pastor, thinking the "lighter demands" afforded greater writing opportunities, which in turn allowed him to impact more people for God's kingdom. Charles Spurgeon, known for his great preaching ability, established a school to mobilize preachers so that more people could hear the gospel. In the twentieth century, Billy Graham humbly measured his impact in terms of those who found their way into meaningful community rather than in terms of the magnitude of those who walked the aisle at his crusades.

These men understood that even though God was working in them in profound ways, it was for the sake of his people and his story, not theirs. It seems obvious, then, that even when God moves in the heart of a leader, he does so to move the hearts of his people. A community of believers following Jesus can image God in ways that an individual simply cannot. The classic passage describing what community looked like in the early church is this:

> And they devoted themselves to the apostles' teaching and the fellowship, to the breaking of bread and the prayers. And awe came upon every soul, and many wonders and signs were being done through the apostles. And all who believed were together

and had all things in common. And they were selling their possessions and belongings and distributing the proceeds to all, as any had need. And day by day, attending the temple together and breaking bread in their homes, they received their food with glad and generous hearts, praising God and having favor with all the people. And the Lord added to their number day by day those who were being saved. (Acts 2:42–47)

do w/ stand out?

The questions to ask about this passage are: What is unique to this community? and, What is to be common of every community that follows Jesus? The ways in which these questions are reconciled have become the building blocks of denominational distinctions. I want to suggest three observable patterns from which many practices can arise. They are worship, belonging, and witness.

Gospel Community Worships

A Gospel Community Is Devoted to Truth

As we observed earlier, biblical worship includes spirit, truth, and love. We find all three present in this description of the early church. Regarding truth, these believers devoted themselves to the apostles' teaching (Acts 2:42) and attended temple daily (v. 46). I am convicted when I read that the early church was devoted to the apostles' teaching. Devotion bespeaks both attitude and habit. These people were not casual observers, or merely acquainted with the teachings of the apostles; these teachings shaped their worldview. It takes hard work to make truth reside at the depths of belief and conviction. Dietrich Bonhoeffer explains the necessity: "The Christian needs another Christian who speaks God's Word to him. He needs him again and again when he becomes uncertain and discouraged, for by himself he cannot help himself without belying the truth."[2] Anyone can acknowledge a truth, but when it moves into the thought and behavior realms of belief and conviction, a truth starts to own you.

Take, for example, the truth of who Jesus is. For Jerusalem residents two thousand years ago, Jesus was a teacher, maybe a candidate for Messiah. Eventually, many saw him as a criminal, for he was executed as public enemy number one. Some were neutral about the identity of Jesus and would have said, "I have seen people who say they believe him to be the son of God, so he must have had some very good things to say." But the reaction was far from neutral in those who heard Peter and Stephen speaking publicly of Jesus, because those speeches made them personally culpable for the execution of Jesus:

> Men of Israel, hear these words: Jesus of Nazareth, a man attested to you by God with mighty works and wonders and signs that God did through him in your midst, as you yourselves know—this Jesus, delivered up according to the definite plan and foreknowledge of God, you crucified and killed by the hands of lawless men. (Acts 2:22–23)

> You stiff-necked people, uncircumcised in heart and ears, you always resist the Holy Spirit. As your fathers did, so do you. Which of the prophets did your fathers not persecute? And they killed those who announced beforehand the coming of the Righteous One, whom you have now betrayed and murdered. (Acts 7:51–52)

The people were forced to deal with Jesus and what has happened; the story was no longer passive data, like a benign news report of a recalled toaster. They had been summoned into the story as participants. Would they leave things as they were and decide Jesus should have died, or would they consider the prophecies? Would they devote themselves to discovering why Jesus is the Promised Righteous One, or would they devote themselves to debunking the prophets' claims? That was the world of the early church. The brand-new believers (more than three thousand, only days old in their faith) were ravenously soaking up all they could about this newfound hero and missing puzzle piece that made sense of the story of God. Gospel community does not settle for truth as informational; it devotes itself to truth as transformational.

A Gospel Community Is Devoted to Prayer

With the early church still in infancy, and the first converts being either Jews or proselytes (Acts 2:11) to the Jewish faith, they still attended temple for prayer services (Acts 3:1). But prayer was more than just part of the services they attended; it was part of their community life (Acts 2:42). Prayer is part of what it means to love God as a worshiper. We learn to communicate with him in prayer. Praying in community is also part of a shared worship experience. Look at two examples of Paul's prayers for different faith communities that he shepherded:

> For this reason I bow my knees before the Father, from whom every family in heaven and on earth is named, that according to the riches of his glory he may grant you to be strengthened with power through his Spirit in your inner being, so that Christ may dwell in your hearts through faith—that you, being rooted and grounded in love, may have strength to comprehend with all the saints what is the breadth and length and height and depth, and to know the love of Christ that surpasses knowledge, that you may be filled with all the fullness of God. Now to him who is able to do far more abundantly than all that we ask or think, according to the power at work within us, to him be glory in the church and in Christ Jesus throughout all generations, forever and ever. Amen. (Eph. 3:14–21)

> And it is my prayer that your love may abound more and more, with knowledge and all discernment, so that you may approve what is excellent, and so be pure and blameless for the day of Christ, filled with the fruit of righteousness that comes through Jesus Christ, to the glory and praise of God. (Phil. 1:9–11)

Do Paul's prayers inspire worship within your spirit? Do they spur you to want to know more about Jesus, to experience his love in more profound ways, and to believe that the life Jesus died to provide is bigger than you were thinking it to be? Would your community look different if you prayed like this for one another, even if you prayed these very prayers? When I read these prayers, I don't know if there was an Ephesian or a Philippian with a runaway donkey, or an exam, or a potential job, but I do know about Jesus and the greatness of the life experience he intends for his followers. Somehow I think we have shrunk our prayer life to to-do lists for God, and we have shrunk our worship life in the process. Here is how Luke describes an unshrunken worshiping heart in Acts 2: "Awe came upon every soul" (v. 43). Gospel community helps fan the flame of awe within the soul by being a worshipful community.

A Gospel Community Breaks Bread Together

Some take the biblical idea of breaking bread together to mean solely the Lord's Table or Communion. Others believe it means that they ate meals together, and still others who do not so easily separate the two think that they observed Communion while eating a meal together. The mode, however, is not the critical component.[3] What does seem to be happening in the community life of the early church is a frequent remembrance of the death of Jesus and his promise to return. The practice no doubt called people to a sobering remembrance of Jesus's death for their sin; it is synonymous with saying that gospel community worships through confession and repentance.

I distinguish these two words, *confession* and *repentance*, because confession is the admitting of sin and repentance is the turning from sin. Most people are remorseful about sin, especially any adverse effects that have happened to them or others. However, confession of sin is coming to God and admitting you have sinned against him and that you have chosen to be the author of a preferred alternate story, which amounts to idolatry. To repent means to do a 180-degree turn from your idol to God (1

Thess. 1:9). While repentance is a matter of mind and heart, it is also a matter of renouncing sin through transformed behavior. Just as sin is committed in the heart and mind as well as in deed, so is loving obedience to Jesus.

It is dangerous and tempting to change behavior without also changing heart and mind. Behavior modification has to do with "religion," not with Christianity, and it leads to judgmentalism. Confession and repentance will not happen in a judgmental community. Gospel community calls people out of their bondage, out of their lies, and out of their mess, but gospel community members are willing to walk with their brothers and sisters through their exodus rather than simply being cheerleaders across the Jordan, hoping they make it to the Promised Land. This means that when someone confesses sin, they are loved. The Bible tells of this being the kind of love God has for us: "For while we were still weak, at the right time Christ died for the ungodly. For one will scarcely die for a righteous person—though perhaps for a good person one would dare even to die—but God shows his love for us in that while we were still sinners, Christ died for us" (Rom. 5:6–8).

Here is where our thinking can high-center, and we can get stuck from truly making disciples. We run to the love of God because it creates a safe place for sinners to confess and repent, and God is quick to forgive those who come broken. "The sacrifices of God are a broken spirit; a broken and contrite heart, O God, you will not despise" (Ps. 51:17). God is also quick to discipline his children, that we may experience righteousness through its training:

> "For the Lord disciplines the one he loves, and chastises every son whom he receives." It is for discipline that you have to endure. God is treating you as sons. For what son is there whom his father does not discipline? If you are left without discipline, in which all have participated, then you are illegitimate children and not sons. Besides this, we have had earthly

fathers who disciplined us and we respected them. Shall we not much more be subject to the Father of spirits and live? For they disciplined us for a short time as it seemed best to them, but he disciplines us for our good, that we may share his holiness. For the moment all discipline seems painful rather than pleasant, but later it yields the peaceful fruit of righteousness to those who have been trained by it. (Heb. 12:6–11)

As these verses relate to community, there is the call for a delicate balance between creating a safe relational place for confession and repentance to happen, and being the loving relational place where discipline happens. It allows community to be an environment in which we image God and behold God imaged one to another. The key component permeating this environment is love.

Gospel Community Is Belonging

God's love as shown in Hebrews 12:6–11 disciplines. In a gospel community, disciples call one another up to the high calling of Christ, which is to image God. Community is not merely about being the people of God, but it is about being a people of God who image their God. The God of the Bible is an eternal, triune community, loving each other and living in worshipful, belonging relationships.

A simple formula for determining communication dynamics within a community is to take the number of people in the community (x) and multiply that by ($x-1$). So applied, within the Trinity there are six communication responsibilities: the Father communicates to the Son and the Spirit, the Son communicates to the Father and the Spirit, and the Spirit communicates to the Father and the Son.[4] This community communicates (Gen. 1:26) and each member explains the others (John 14:8–9) to those outside the community. Jesus longed to return to sharing in the glory of God that he experienced with the Father before his incarnation (John 17:4–5).

We know about this eternal community primarily from how they interact with one another. *The Father, the Son,* and *begotten* are words that describe the relationship between Jesus and the Father within the community. Both Jesus and the Holy Spirit are described as advocates for believers (1 John 2:1; Rom. 8:26–27). While it is wonderful to know this about their relationship to us, it is helpful to know it regarding their relationship with the Father. The book of Job gives us an example of the kind of slander the Devil brings before God against those who follow God (Job 1:8–11). It is awesome to think that while someone estranged from God (the Devil) is accusing me, two persons within the Godhead, two members of the eternal community, are championing me. Apart from the Father listening to the Son and the Spirit advocate and intercede, there would be no one to declare our redemption and transformation.

John 13 provides a tremendous picture of Jesus's giving and modeling community to his disciples:

> Now before the Feast of the Passover, when Jesus knew that his hour had come to depart out of this world to the Father, having loved his own who were in the world, he loved them to the end. During supper, when the devil had already put it into the heart of Judas Iscariot, Simon's son, to betray him, Jesus, knowing that the Father had given all things into his hands, and that he had come from God and was going back to God, rose from supper. He laid aside his outer garments, and taking a towel, tied it around his waist. Then he poured water into a basin and began to wash the disciples' feet and to wipe them with the towel that was wrapped around him. He came to Simon Peter, who said to him, "Lord, do you wash my feet?" Jesus answered him, "What I am doing you do not understand now, but afterward you will understand." Peter said to him, "You shall never wash my feet." Jesus answered him, "If I do not wash you, you have no share with me." Simon Peter said to him, "Lord, not my feet only but also my hands and my head!" Jesus said to him, "The one who has bathed

does not need to wash, except for his feet, but is completely clean. And you are clean, but not every one of you." For he knew who was to betray him; that was why he said, "Not all of you are clean." When he had washed their feet and put on his outer garments and resumed his place, he said to them, "Do you understand what I have done to you? You call me Teacher and Lord, and you are right, for so I am. If I then, your Lord and Teacher, have washed your feet, you also ought to wash one another's feet. For I have given you an example, that you also should do just as I have done to you. Truly, truly, I say to you, a servant is not greater than his master, nor is a messenger greater than the one who sent him. If you know these things, blessed are you if you do them. I am not speaking of all of you; I know whom I have chosen. But the Scripture will be fulfilled, 'He who ate my bread has lifted his heel against me.' I am telling you this now, before it takes place, that when it does take place you may believe that I am he. Truly, truly, I say to you, whoever receives the one I send receives me, and whoever receives me receives the one who sent me." (vv. 1–20)

Look at the interaction between Jesus and Peter. Peter objects to Jesus's washing his feet. Jesus will later tell Peter that Peter does not understand what Jesus is doing. This means Jesus was obviously doing something other than foot washing. Dealing with Peter's objections, Jesus goes on to tell him that if he does not wash his feet, Peter will have no share in him. Upon hearing that, Peter, true to his impulsiveness, tells Jesus to give him the whole five-star washing, including head and hands. Jesus then tells Peter that Peter is clean but that he needs a tune-up because feet get dirty in travel. Jesus drives this whole lesson home a bit more by saying, "If I then, your Lord and Teacher, have washed your feet, you also ought to wash one another's feet" (v. 14). In the ᶜ this rather cryptic conversation, I think it is safe to say talking about forgiveness. The cleansing that had ed was Peter's rebirth, the beginning of his being e image of Jesus. Nevertheless, within a few short hours of this meal, Peter would deny Jesus, Judas would betray Jesus, and the other ten would desert Jesus.

The eleven needed a paradigm of how to recover from distorting the grace given them; in essence, how to rebound from sin. The model Jesus gives is community, a place to acknowledge sin, to confess it as wrong, and to make things right. Foot washing is not an issue of eternal destination; it is about relationship. To the person who has experienced oneness with Jesus, there are few pains as unsettling as sinful discord. If we have champions in Jesus and the Holy Spirit before the Father, we should certainly be able to champion one another within our communities. In fact, it is a way we image God, for we get the opportunity to forgive as Jesus forgave (Col. 3:13) and to advocate for one another in similar fashion to Jesus and the Holy Spirit. This cannot happen, however, if confession, repentance, truth, and accountability are not part of a community's DNA.

It is important to note the difference between belonging in a community and communism. I heard a lecture by Francis Schaeffer in which he said that communism stole its basic paradigm from God's kingdom; it just removed the king, which makes it functionally attractive while being theologically heretical. I have heard many people try to use Acts 2:44–45 as the basis for which to establish communism in their community.

In Acts 5, we read of a couple who sold their property and lied about the portion they gave to the church. Their motive was to be esteemed as Joseph had been when he gave his sacrificial gift (Acts 4:36–37). "But Peter said, 'Ananias, why has Satan filled your heart to lie to the Holy Spirit and to keep back for yourself part of the proceeds of the land? While it remained unsold, did it not remain your own? And after it was sold, was it not at your disposal? Why is it that you have contrived this deed in your heart? You have not lied to men but to God'" (Acts 5:3–4). Peter told Ananias that the property was his before and after the sale, and that the money was his own to steward. I want to use these verses to answer the questions we posed at the beginning of the chapter: what is unique to this early-church community and what is to be common of every community that follows Jesus?

Certainly loving concern, benevolence, and mercy are to be common, but the description of brothers holding all things in common—selling and distributing to each as they have need—is illustrative more than it is prescriptive for community life. The fact that I will share my life with other believers means it must go beyond a weekly meeting, beyond a geographic or affinity connection. The fact that those in the early church sacrificially helped one another and were in each other's homes on a daily basis indicates a lifestyle. The fact that Christian community is meant to model the Trinity means that community is at the very core of gospel identity. We profoundly belong to one another as the family of God. This truth must disrupt us at the core of individualism, resetting us to what it means to love another as Jesus loved (John 13:34).

Gospel Community Is Witness

Imagine what this new community looked like. There had to be a buzz about these people who were sharing meals, selling property, and worshiping Jesus. Luke describes the impact this community had on the everyday lives of observers as "having favor with all the people. And the Lord added to their number day by day those who were being saved" (Acts 2:47). This description is mentioned in terms of fruit or effects. Favor with others is something the Lord is said to provide.[5] When we try to engineer it, we are in danger of pride or of falling into "the fear of man."

Luke's second descriptor is that "the Lord added to their number day by day those who were being saved." Again we see terms of fruitfulness. Jesus was quick to point out, in John 15, that fruitfulness is not within our control. He describes himself as the vine and the Father as the vinedresser (v. 1). It becomes clear through Jesus's description of the vine and the careful pruning of the vinedresser that the fruit is managed. We, as branches, have the privilege and responsibility of abiding in Jesus. It is clear from this description of gospel community that living in community images God to a world in a way that independent living cannot.

Jesus describes this in John 17:21 as he prays for us to love one another, "that they may all be one, just as you, Father, are in me, and I in you, that they also may be in us, so that the world may believe that you have sent me." Jesus believed that our oneness was convincing proof that Jesus was who he claimed to be—sent from the Father as the Savior of the world. Fishing during Jesus's day was done with nets. There does seem to be evidence that fishermen worked individually, but for the most part fishing was done in teams. The net was lowered and gathered back up by several fishermen. When Jesus called his disciples to follow him, he told them that they were to be fishers of men. As they considered his metaphor, rods and reels would not have come to mind, but rather boats, nets, and cooperative community working toward a common goal. What this means for a gospel community is learning how to live together in redemptive rhythms.

Some people in your community may be extremely connected and gifted in connecting to their unbelieving neighbors. Rather than admiring them and leaving them to fish on their own, community learns how to fish together. Tim Chester and Steve Timmis explain the value of evangelism taking place in community: "By making evangelism a community project, it also takes seriously the sovereign work of the Holy Spirit in distributing a variety of gifts among his people."[6] Jesus uses another analogy of harvesting that suggests a diversity of assignments:

Do you not say, "There are yet four months, then comes the harvest"? Look, I tell you, lift up your eyes, and see that the fields are white for harvest. Already the one who reaps is receiving wages and gathering fruit for eternal life, so that sower and reaper may rejoice together. For here the saying holds true, "One sows and another reaps." I sent you to reap that for which you did not labor. Others have labored, and you have entered into their labor. (John 4:35–38)

Jesus was telling his disciples that some people sow while others are present when what was sown comes to fruition. This should encourage each of us to realize that being on mission is not about getting people to make decisions for Christ. It is about imaging God in such a way that Jesus is seen for who he is.

Communities, therefore, are witnesses in that they show what the kingdom of God is meant to look like. "It is our cross-love for each other that proclaims the truth of the gospel to a watching and skeptical world," writes Chester and Timmis. "In our experience people are often attracted to the Christian community before they are attracted to the Christian message."[7] They model grace, love, forgiveness, truth, and identity. Believers imaging God in community image God best. Look at this list of things we are to show another:

- Love: "People will know that you are my disciples, if you have love for one another" (John 13:35).
- Peace: "Be at peace among yourselves" (1 Thess. 5:13).
- Hospitality: "Show hospitality to one another without grumbling" (1 Pet. 4:9).
- Service: "For you were called to freedom, brothers. Only do not use your freedom as an opportunity for the flesh, but through love serve one another" (Gal. 5:13).
- Instruction: "I myself am satisfied about you, my brothers, that you yourselves are full of goodness, filled with all knowledge and able to instruct one another" (Rom. 15:14).
- Care: "That there may be no division in the body, but that the members may have the same care for one another" (1 Cor. 12:25).
- Forgiveness: "Bearing with one another and, if one has a complaint against another, forgiving each other; as the Lord has forgiven you, so you also must forgive" (Col. 3:13).

- Kindness: "Be kind to one another, tenderhearted, forgiving one another, as God in Christ forgave you" (Eph. 4:32).
- Submission: "Submitting to one another out of reverence for Christ" (Eph. 5:21).
- Honesty: "Do not lie to one another, seeing that you have put off the old self with its practices" (Col. 3:9).

This gives you the idea that gospel community is nothing short of imaging God one to another. This means mirroring to others the transformation that Jesus is doing in each of us individually. This means championing Jesus and the Holy Spirit. This means being a community that calls for sin to be dealt with rather than excused.

Look at yet another time when Jesus confronted Peter, while leaving the door open for him to experience community: "'Simon, Simon, behold, Satan demanded to have you, that he might sift you like wheat, but I have prayed for you that your faith may not fail. And when you have turned again, strengthen your brothers.' Peter said to him, 'Lord, I am ready to go with you both to prison and to death.' Jesus said, 'I tell you, Peter, the rooster will not crow this day, until you deny three times that you know me.'" (Luke 22:31–34).

Jesus warned Peter that he was going to be spiritually attacked. One of the most amazing things about these verses is that Jesus prayed for Peter's faith and for his recovery after it failed. I get so busy praying that I and the people I care about will not sin, that I do not pray for a resilient faith and a God-honoring rebound from sin. Peter responds to Jesus with a prideful swagger, pledging to follow unwaveringly to prison and to death. Perhaps Peter was implying that he would follow even if no one else in the community did. Jesus called Peter to community thinking by saying, "When you have turned again, strengthen your brothers" (v. 32). The opposite of community thinking is competitive thinking.

For Peter to grade himself on a curve, thinking he was a good disciple because he didn't see a better one, was dangerous thinking. Jesus was saying that a good disciple is one who takes his community's health as an assignment, not as a source of identity. There are many disciples who feel that they are good Christians because they go to a good church, and others who think they are good Christians because they know many Christians who are less committed than they are. Neither mindset catches the spirit of gospel community, whereas both reflect the spirit of consumerism. The first "consumes" a right standing by hitchhiking onto the work, gifts, or obedience of others. The second "consumes" a right standing by having a better résumé than others'. This comparative thinking serves only to advance the kind of self-righteous spirit that Peter blurted out when he said, "Lord, I am ready to go with you both to prison and to death" (v. 33).

Jesus calls each of us to community, but the way to experience and express community is through worship, belonging, and witness, calling one another to the hope resident within Jesus's call to follow him.

CHAPTER 7 ASSIGNMENT

Exploring Biblical Community

1) Read Genesis 2:15–25. In what ways is marriage supposed to be an environment for experiencing community?
2) Read Matthew 18:15–20. What role does community play in church discipline?
3) Read Acts 20:17–38. What elements of community do you see demonstrated between Paul and the Ephesian elders?
4) Read Philippians 2:1–5. How does Paul describe the bond of Christian community?
5) Read 1 Corinthians 13. There are two distinct lists here: what love does and what love does not do. How can you be more loving in your community?

Digging Deeper

Reflect upon how these verses inform us as to what biblical community looks like.

"Be at peace with one another" (Mark 9:50).

"Wash one another's feet" (John 13:14).

"Love one another" (John 13:34–35; 15:12, 17).

"Owe no one anything, except to love each other" (Rom. 13:8).

"Love one another with brotherly affection. Outdo one another in showing honor" (Rom. 12:10).

"Live in harmony with one another" (Rom. 12:16).

"Let us not pass judgment on one another any longer" (Rom. 14:13).

"Welcome one another as Christ has welcomed you" (Rom. 15:7).

"Greet one another with a holy kiss" (Rom. 16:16; 1 Cor. 16:20, 2 Cor. 13:12; 1 Thess. 5:26).

"When you come together to eat, wait for one another" (1 Cor. 11:33).

"Members may have the same care for one another" (1 Cor. 12:25).

"Through love serve one another" (Gal. 5:13).

"Bear one another's burdens" (Gal. 6:2).

"If you bite and devour one another, watch out that you are not consumed by one another" (Gal. 5:15).

"Let us not become conceited, provoking . . . [and] envying one another" (Gal. 5:26).

" . . . with all humility and gentleness, with patience, bearing with one another in love" (Eph. 4:2).

"Be kind to one another, tenderhearted, forgiving one another" (Eph. 4:32).

" . . . addressing one another in psalms and hymns and spiritual songs, singing and making melody to the Lord with your heart" (Eph. 5:19).

" . . . submitting to one another out of reverence for Christ" (Eph. 5:21).

"Do not lie to one another" (Col. 3:9).

" . . . bearing with one another" (Col. 3:13).

"If one has a complaint against another, forgiving each other" (Col. 3:13).

"Let the word of Christ dwell in you richly . . . admonishing one another" (Col. 3:16).

"May the Lord make you increase and abound in love for one another" (1 Thess. 3:12).

"Encourage one another" (1 Thess. 4:18, 5:11; Heb. 10:25).

"Build one another up" (1 Thess. 5:11).

"Exhort one another every day" (Heb. 3:13).

"Let us consider how to stir up one another to love and good works" (Heb. 10:24).

8

COMMUNITY DISTORTIONS

Most people will sign off on the need for a group to help them pursue their goals. People face the decision of whether to join a group almost daily, be it online, at work, after work, before work, for health, or for lack of health, or to eat right, exercise, read a book, write a book, walk, jog, or run. Group options seem endless.

So what is the big deal about making sure we live in community? And why do we seem to have a hunger pang for vulnerable connection? Even a cursory reading of the Bible shows the gospel is not a solo event. Only in a consumer culture could a privatized view of "Jesus dying just for me so that I can go to heaven" emerge as the gospel. Listening to Jesus's words describing the poor, the meek, and the peacemakers, or seeing just how much of our English Bible's translation of "you" is plural when it describes gospel transformation, should recalibrate our view of salvation from being personally graced to being graced in order to be a source of grace to others. The degree to which this will happen depends on whether we live relationally or individualistically. An isolated life is one of insulated grace. Conversely, connected hearts distribute grace.

Often, our need or desire to be graced causes us to distort community. It is our wants or felt needs that tend to motivate us to join a group in the first place. But it is absurd to think that seven to twelve people can come together and form a group to meet their personal needs yet wind up with a communal and others-focused byproduct. It seems safe to conclude that most distortions are born and bred in the *why* of forming or joining the group.

Distortion 1: Community as Therapy

Tom joined a group for men who struggle with pornography. Tom didn't see himself as a sex addict. He had simply grown up with pornographic materials around his house, and now he was getting serious with a woman, and she had told him that his pornography habit was a deal breaker to their relationship. Tom found the group of men amazingly transparent, and the leader was good at getting them to be honest. When I met with Tom, he had been attending the group for eighteen months. His behaviors had altered, his girlfriend had become his fiancée, and he seemed to be maturing. Tom came to see me because he felt that he really didn't need the group anymore, but he really felt connected to the guys; they were his friends. He told me, "I almost feel that I need to sin so I can stay in the group and keep my friends."

This is a walloping distortion of gospel community. It is great to connect, to call one another out on sin, and to ask one another to be vulnerable. It is tragic, however, to need to be "sick" to belong to the club. When a group centers on a problem rather than on the gospel, members have to keep their problems to stay in the group. However, when a group centers on Jesus and the gospel, people can stay in the group as long as they desire to see the gospel transform them into the likeness of Jesus.

Even if a group is formed around an interest or need, the group comes apart when its focus is self-serving, pain-focused, or recovery-centered. If you lead a group that is recovery-centered, you have probably noticed high dropout rates and you may even have designed entrance and exit ramps to your group. It can be helpful to have intense times as a group that deal with habitual sin, destructive attitudes, or life-stage issues such as pre-marriage and parenting, but they quickly become dysfunctional when members get identity from the issue that brought them to the group.

Therapeutic components that are helpful to a group include a safe environment where people can share without fear of rejection or breach of confidentiality; a discovery environment where members can connect the dots between truths and distortions that have formed their dysfunctional framework for interpreting life; and a hope environment where members are encouraged to experience freedom, which is way more life-giving than behavior management or abstinence.

Distortion 2: Community as Network

Networks are formed for the purpose of resourcing one another's agendas. Take, for example, a local chamber of commerce. It functions as a place where local business owners come together and promote services or events that may be of use to one another. They may also come together to discuss how to address an issue that impacts their businesses, such as a major street being closed for repair or a new zoning by the city. However, at a network meeting, members do not come together to speak into one another's lives or to find partners to journey through life together.

Some community groups function way more like a network than like a life-formation community. The gatherings are social, conversation is casual, and people may offer lightweight assistance to one another, such as if one member's car breaks down and another member has a brother who is a mechanic and will provide a good deal. For the most part, networks are built on the premise that members have a strength or asset that they will bring to the table and that together they can do more than they can on their own. The goal is to leverage their individual strengths so that all in the group can get what they want.

Community has a different objective. Community is most profound when members are able to bring their weaknesses rather than their strengths to the table. When someone miscarries, loses a job, or gets the news of a life-altering disease, and relationally connected distributers of grace are there for one another, community is experienced. When God-given gifts are used to build up the body, such as encouragement, hospitality, and giving, group members start to discern the difference between leveraging pooled assets and being agents of grace.

When a woman calls the group leader and says, "My husband didn't come home last night, and when I talked to him on the phone today, he said that he had spent the night with a man," the men from her community group talk to her husband, confront him with his sin, and offer to walk with him and his family in bringing gospel transformation to bear. Such a community is radically different from a network that tries to provide the woman with tools for demanding her rights. A gospel community will function redemptively and will serve as family to one another. Joseph Hellerman explains, "No biblical image of the atonement has greater potential to resonate with our relationally broken culture than the good news that we can be reconciled to God and to our fellow human beings through the death of Jesus on the cross."[1] Community means you are willing to travel at the pace of the slowest sheep, based on Jesus's willingness to step down on our behalf (Phil. 2:5–11).

Distortion 3: Community as Program

Groups are composed of humans, but a group of humans imaging God, worshiping God in community on mission, is more than human. Such a group is the body of Christ. It is a tragedy when groups that are composed of people supernaturally birthed into the life of Jesus and inhabited by the Holy Spirit see their gatherings as a programmed event. Several studies have been conducted in search for the qualities that contribute to healthy gospel communities.

One benchmark of health within a gospel community is the frequency of interaction between members outside programmed events. If a group meets on Tuesday nights, do its members get together during other times of the week as well? Do they socialize and help one another meet life's ongoing demands on a regular basis outside of the Tuesday meeting? If its members see each other only on Tuesday nights, the gathering is most likely a humanly programmed event.

Programmed groups also tend to hold discussions that are more informational than transformational. If a small-group Bible study decides to discuss the biblical passage covered in last week's sermon, the questions and discussion should aim at moving from neat to messy. The interaction between members will not go beyond what feels safe if the context for the gathering has a "meeting" sort of feel. Members ought to see themselves as agents of grace—Jesus's arms, mouth, and legs, each calling the others to repentance, faith, confession, reconciliation, and love. Community is not simply a human event. Community is way more than the practical outworking of managing our behaviors and objectives; community is the vehicle through which saving grace is released.[2]

Most of us have goals, and some of us have even set those goals into action with plans and patterns of behavior, but realistically, more times than not, the reason we have set a goal, especially in an area that needs improvement, is that there is a truth distortion associated with the area of our goal. For example, if you have set a goal to exercise and become better physically fit this year, you might have been motivated by some distorted thinking about physical fitness. I grew up constantly involved in sports. In high school I played on several different varsity teams; in college I wrestled, and in my forties I ran the Chicago Marathon. But my thinking is distorted—I think I am an athlete and that I am in good physical shape. The truth is that I have a desk job, I am over fifty, and I am a grandfather.

One spring recently, I decided to undertake a training program in hopes of participating in a race by fall. After about six weeks, I developed a condition called "plantar fasciitis," which sidelined me for almost three months. During that time, I gained weight, which caused me to have back pain. The sad truth is that I am not an athlete. I have to set goals for weight control and health, because my distorted view of my physical conditioning allows me too much freedom in my eating habits, and it drives me to train with a far too aggressive timeline.

Let's move a little deeper into the soul as we consider the following scenario. John seldom shares his feelings with his wife. He comes home from work, dives in front of the television, and is not heard from again until it is time to go to bed. It is actually a labor for him to go to community group because it means he misses some great shows, and recording them just stacks him up on his viewing for another night. One night at community group, John admitted that he could share himself a bit more with his wife. His care group leader welcomed this comment from John and asked him, "What keeps you from sharing the deep things of your soul with your wife?"

John expected to be congratulated for his transparency, not drilled to the point of vulnerability. A couple of the men were praying under their breath that this would be the breakthrough of the night. John's wife was hoping he would not withdraw. For some reason, John stepped into the question pitched by his leader and swung for the fence: "I am hiding. I escape into television shows, computer games, and household projects. You name it—if there is a way for me not to think or share, I take it."

His wife just about fell off her chair, and the men intensified their prayers. The leader looked at John's wife, Shelly, and asked her, "What would it be like if John were to share his thoughts with you?"

Shelly almost cried as she said, "I would feel like he loved me."

John looked at her and asked, "Don't you feel like I love you?"

Shelly then told John she feels like he cares for her but that he didn't trust her enough to let her care for him. She tells him that it feels like he is hiding all the time and that she has interpreted that as a lack of trust on his part, which has hurt her.

One of the guys who had been praying said, "Can we pray for the two of you right now? John, can you love Shelly this week by not turning on the television and not hiding from her but by talking to her?" The group went in to a time of prayer for the couple, and the couple went home from something that was not simply human.

During the following week John got a couple of calls from guys saying that they were praying that he will have the courage to unplug the television and engage Shelly as his life's partner. John's community group leader met John for breakfast and asked John more questions to help him discover his distortions. After thinking and praying about the questions, John arrived at home after work with something to share with Shelly. A couple of Shelly's friends from community group made a point to see her during the week to help her encourage John without nagging him. After a couple of weeks of coaching and support, John and Shelly thanked the group for their "intrusion" into their lives and said that the group had helped them out of a hole in which they had seemed to be stuck.

This was more than behavior management. This kind of interaction and support requires living life together, not just attending a program. Even in this simple, quick-fix illustration, prayer and dependence upon the Holy Spirit to see something happen were involved. Hopefully, this gives you an idea of how distorted we are in our thinking when we only go to Tuesday night meetings without also living together in community.

Distortion 4: Community as Exclusively Christian

Sometimes, when a group forms around an affinity, things like communication, understanding, and sensitivity to one another's circumstances, things slide. When snowboarders form a group, the lingo they use can sometimes sound foreign to a non-boarder. The same can happen if a group is primarily Christian. Those who are not Christian or are new in their faith can feel alienated just because of language and mannerisms. If someone says, "We went to the doctor this week, and we found out we are expecting. God is so good!" most people will get the gist of what's being said, but it is sloppy Christianity to make God good because we got good news. Those who do not know God may wonder how bad things have to get in the world for God to be bad. Those who buy in to a good God because of good things are being set up for a faith crisis when a really bad thing such as death or cancer hits close to home.

Distorting truth through the words we use keeps a group from being a place for members to bring non-Christians, because they cannot trust what other group members might say. It is wise to keep our thinking and vocabulary precise and real. This doesn't mean that we establish heresy police, but it does mean that we encourage one another to speak truth and to grow in wisdom and understanding of the implications of our words and deeds.

Something else that can cause harm is to allow an "us versus them" mentality to take root within the group. If the members start to fear that new members or visitors will prevent transformational openness, the leader needs to shepherd the group through this distortion. There isn't a better apologetic for unbelievers than to catch believers being transparent with one another. Jesus said that the world will know he is who he claimed to be because of our love for one another (John 17:21).

The life of the Christian community is part of the way in which the gospel is communicated. Lesslie Newbigin describes the local congregation as "the hermeneutic of the gospel"; it is the way in which people understand the gospel.[3] We need to be communities of love. And we need to be *seen* to be communities of love. People need to encounter the church as a network of rela-

tionships rather than as a meeting to attend or a place to enter.[4]
How is the world to see this love if they are not welcomed into
our community settings?

The body of Christ being the body of Christ is an evangelistic
tool in the hands of God. This is not the same as being missional,
which is to engage culture and take the gospel to a context other
than church; here, we are talking about making church be a
place where the gospel is practiced as embodied values. We can
do this with the hope that an onlooker or an estranged believer
will experience the convicting work of the Holy Spirit, prompt-
ing him to want to be part of something loving, redemptive, and
supernatural. This makes a community with an observable faith
inclusive, rather than exclusive, to those who *are* not engaged.

This kind of community is not calling for conformity.
Conformity has way more to do with outer adjustments and
learned behavior. As we have just warned, we do not want to
adopt learned behaviors and ghetto language that keep outsiders in the dark; rather, we want to create an environment in
which people can observe believers lovingly calling one another
to repent and transform, prayerfully interceding for one another
so that true healing might take place, and dealing with the disap-
pointments of living in a kingdom that is not yet fully realized.
This goes far beyond countering culture with acceptance; this
is more about creating a culture. This is a culture that values
people as image bearers of God, while knowing each of us is ruin-
ously marred by sin and must be remade in the image of Jesus.
It sees that each of us is a worshiper, but left to ourselves we
would worship creation rather than the Creator, so we help one
another walk away from idols that ruin us. We create a culture
that sparks imagination to dream the grand vision of what life
in Jesus can be like when we speak truth in love to one another.
Community is life on life rather than a programmed pod of motivated speakers achieving "greater things."

Community, then, is easily distorted and shrunken into manageable meetings with codes of conduct, expectations, and compartmental sound bites. This certainly is not what it looked like when Jesus lived with his disciples. When we base community on the nature of God as Trinity, we understand that it must issue out of our person and be ruthlessly protected from degenerating to program. Bruce Ware cautions us that "to miss [community patterned after our triune God] is to miss part of the wonder of human life, and it stems from failing to see something more of the wonder of God himself."[5] Community distortions prevent us from experiencing and expressing the salvation Jesus died to provide.

CHAPTER 8 ASSIGNMENT

Exploring Community Distortions

    1) Look at the qualities of kingdom members described by Jesus in Matthew 5:2–12. How do they differ when read from both individualistic and community perspectives?

    2) Read Matthew 23:13–29. Jesus gives religious distorters severe warnings. Put these distortions into your own words as they would read if committed by you or others.

    3) Read 1 Corinthians 11:17–34. How did the Corinthian church distort community?

    4) Read Galatians 2:11–14. What about Peter's behavior did Paul think was not in step with the truth of the gospel?

    5) Read Paul's letter to Philemon. What is Paul asking Philemon to do? What is the basis for Paul's request? What challenges to community can you discern in this letter?

Digging Deeper

The following verses identify many actions and attitudes that destroy community. Summarize your observations into threats or distortions.

Psalm 5:9

Psalm 50:16–18

Psalm 101:5, 7

Proverbs 6:16–19

Proverbs 11:2–3

Proverbs 14:6–9

Proverbs 15:32

Proverbs 17:5

Proverbs 20:1

Proverbs 21:13

Matthew 6:1–7, 16

Matthew 7:1–5

Matthew 15:7

Luke 18:9–14

1 Corinthians 5:9–13
Galatians 3:1–9
1 Timothy 4:1–3
James 3:16
1 Peter 2:1

9

MISSION

The story of God is inherently *missional*. The very reason we are aware of his story and are invited in is that God is by nature a gracious and redeeming God. His story tells of his costly mission to rescue those who have rebelled against his right to be the hero of the story, which includes them. This rescue venture, including righting the rebellion and establishing the harmony of his kingdom, is the mission at the heart of his story.

What Is Precious to God?

Since it is God's heart that establishes the right and wrong of the story, let's focus on what is precious to him.

His Glory

As we have already seen, each member of the Trinity loves the others. They enjoy intimate community with one another, and each delights when the other receives worship. Look at the description Jesus gives of his interaction with the Father:

> So Jesus said to them, "Truly, truly, I say to you, the Son can do nothing of his own accord, but only what he sees the Father doing. For whatever the Father does, that the Son does likewise. For the Father loves the Son and shows him all that he himself is doing. And greater works than these will he show him, so that you may marvel. For as the Father raises the dead and gives them life, so also the Son gives life to whom he will. The Father judges no one, but has given all judgment to the

Son, that all may honor the Son, just as they honor the Father. Whoever does not honor the Son does not honor the Father who sent him." (John 5:19–23)

When Jesus describes the working of the Trinity in his incarnation, he cannot neatly separate what the Father does from what the Son does, and there is no meaningful context for the Son's being on the planet apart from the Father's sending him. The Father was willing to send his Son to earth and die that the glory of God would be declared by a redeemed people. The Son was willing to come to earth and die a brutal and wicked death that the glory of God might be declared through those for whom he died. And the Spirit is willing to take Jesus's place as the comforter, making a holy people who, through his transforming work, can comprehend the things of God for the glory of God (John 16:7–15; 1 Cor. 2:7–14). Commenting on John's Gospel, Andreas Köstenberger writes that "the Spirit is a living Presence who applies Jesus' work to the world through representatives: by teaching and reminding them of Jesus' words (14:26; 16:13–14), by bearing witness to Jesus (15:26), and by convicting the world of its unbelief (16:8–11)."[1]

If we think that the primary motivation for God's rescue is to keep rebels from hell, we miss the point of the rescue. I have had many conversations with people who object to the thought that they are not 100 percent free-willed agents. The argument usually goes something like this: "If I am to truly love God, then I must be truly free to either choose or reject God." What I find fascinating about this line of thinking is its complacency with the options. Would you like to choose God and live a completely pleasant life in heaven for eternity, or would you like to reject God and die a perfectly miserable death in a place of eternal torment forever? How can anyone feel like they were given a "free" moral choice with those two options?[2] There is never really an option. Hell, torment, and punishment don't sound like they need much of a pro and con evaluation worksheet.

If a man were to hold a mother at gunpoint and demand that she must decide between having her children shot before her eyes or leaving her family and running away with him, she will choose to run away with the man. Does this woman make the choice of her own free will? If people are faced with the choice between hell and running away with Jesus, is that really a choice?

The point I am trying to make here is that the saving work of God is rooted far deeper in the glory of God than in the lost state of a human heart. This is why the gospel makes sense for today, before you die. It is not as much about escaping hell as it is about glorifying or imaging God. In fact, since the Father, Son, and Holy Spirit all sacrificed greatly for this epic rescue, it would be impossible for us to image God without great sacrifice. Jesus did not pull back from the bold demands he was making on the lives of those who would call him Lord: "Jesus told his disciples, 'If anyone would come after me, let him deny himself and take up his cross and follow me'" (Matt. 16:24; cf. Luke 14:33–35). The glory of God is why we are willing to die to self, and glorifying God is what everyone is called to do in his story. To refuse to image the glory of God is to live as a rebel within his story.

His People

Having said that the glory of God is at the heart of the story, it is important to understand that God has indeed told a story, and he tells it through the redemptive work he does in the hearts and lives of his people. Therefore, the people of God are precious to God not just because we are useful to him but because he loves us and shares life-giving purpose with us as image bearers. While God has good works prepared for us to do, it is in community that we find synergy in being witnesses. As we saw in chapter 7, love can be observed and grace can be expressed and experienced, and transformation looks like family calling one another to our hope in Jesus (1 John 3:1–3; Heb. 10:24–25). It is pleasing to God when we live out his transforming with one another in the midst of a distorted humanity (Eph. 1:3–10). Greg Beale determines that "our task as the covenant community, the church is to be God's temple, so filled with his glorious presence that we expand and fill the earth with that presence until God finally accomplishes the goal completely at the end of time!"[3] Jesus is our model of what the story of God looks like: he lived in relationship with disciples (Luke 22:28), he mourned the death of a friend (John 11:33–38), and he brought acceptance to those who had experienced rejection (Luke 7:36–50).

Each person with his spiritual gifts and talents is like a tube of a particular color of paint. Squeezed onto a pallet with other paint colors, each takes on complementary combinations and contrasts. It takes the canvas of mission, however, where love and truth are worshipfully imaged through a redeemed people in a fallen world for the brushstrokes of grace to be given artistic expression of beauty.

His Creation

Creation is precious to God, as well. Consider how he refers to it as a display of his wisdom and power (Job 38), or how he depicts himself as incomparable as the creator and sustainer of the world, including its ecosystem and the affairs of history (Isaiah 40). These are not displays of pride or statements of dominance. God has made his creation (including humans) in such a way that his fingerprints are discernable. Calvin observes that "wherever you turn your eyes, there is no portion of the world, however minute, that does not exhibit at least some sparks of beauty; while it is impossible to contemplate the vast and beautiful fabric as it extends around, without being overwhelmed by the immense weight of glory."[4] These fingerprints are of a mighty and gentle, wise and simple, and orderly and spontaneous God, and of a God bigger than his creation, yet so involved in it. This kind of God was not imagined or invented by humans. God graciously reveals himself through his creation to his creation, and it delights him to do so. This provides a theology for our stewardship of creation, because it is something precious and pleasing to him.[5] It also provides a theology for mercy ministries, because people as God's creation are valued by him as his image bearers.[6]

The Effects of Sin

The Glory of God Is Obscured by Sin

Paul longs for redemption to be complete: "For now we see in a mirror dimly, but then face to face. Now I know in part; then I shall know fully, even as I have been fully known" (1 Cor. 13:12). Using imaging language and the metaphor of a mirror, he looks forward to the time when Jesus will return and do the final righting of all sin's damage. For now, however, we still see in a mirror dimly. Many of the mirrors used in biblical times were polished brass; a mirror could lose its luster and crisp reflective qualities, leaving only vague or distorted images. In a reference to the great salvation God gives, he calls the Holy Spirit a deposit or a guarantee of a coming, full inheritance (2 Cor. 1:21; Eph. 1:14). Sin has distorted our hearts from being accurate receptors of the glory of God, the curse still covers creation, and the works of the Devil still exist (2 Cor. 4:4). This accounts for why God's precious glory is displayed in ways less than he originally intended.

The People of God Are Distorted by Sin

When we consider how sin still lingers on the earth and in our lives, we realize what a miracle it is that God is seen at all in the lives and community of his people. James wrote to first-century believers and told them how their sin hindered their prayers:

> You desire and do not have, so you murder. You covet and can-not obtain, so you fight and quarrel. You do not have, because you do not ask. You ask and do not receive, because you ask wrongly, to spend it on your passions. You adulterous people! Do you not know that friendship with the world is enmity with

God? Therefore whoever wishes to be a friend of the world makes himself an enemy of God. (James 4:2–4)

It's not so much that God is angry with our selfish prayers and says no. It's that selfish prayers are not prayed for the glory of God or even for the ongoing telling of the story. Selfish prayers amount to our asking God to grant us his grace to worship our idols.

Paul prophesies a time when people will live "having the appearance of godliness, but denying its power" (2 Tim. 3:5). When the power of God is missing from the people of God, they have ceased to be the people of God. The power of God can take on many forms, but it is safe to say that if God is not manifesting his presence in discernable ways, if there are no evidences of grace within your faith community, then the very nature of being the people of God is being distorted by sin. There is an inspiring power when the saving and transforming work of God is observed or shared among the community of God's people. Paul commends the Thessalonians for their display of the gospel in their transformation and mercy toward others:

> Our gospel came to you not only in word, but also in power and in the Holy Spirit and with full conviction. You know what kind of men we proved to be among you for your sake. And you became imitators of us and of the Lord, for you received the word in much affliction, with the joy of the Holy Spirit, so that you became an example to all the believers in Macedonia and in Achaia. For not only has the word of the Lord sounded forth from you in Macedonia and Achaia, but your faith in God has gone forth everywhere, so that we need not say anything. For they themselves report concerning us the kind of reception we had among you, and how you turned to God from idols to serve the living and true God. (1 Thess. 1:5–9)

Paul tells the Philippians that living in a fallen world with a gospel attitude is a powerful witness: "Do all things without grumbling or questioning, that you may be blameless and innocent, children of God without blemish in the midst of a crooked and twisted generation, among whom you shine as lights in the world" (Phil. 2:14–15).

Taking these three examples and putting them in the dampening context of sin, we see that sin causes the people of God to go amiss in their prayer life and look as though they are praying to a powerless or absent God. When believers persist in sin and do not evidence transformation, the spread of the gospel is hindered. If the people of God do the things of God yet with complaining and arguing, they lose their illuminating qualities in a world of darkness. These are just a few examples in Scripture of how sin can keep us from being the source of delight God desires from his people.

The Creation of God Is Under Sin's Curse

Paul describes creation as groaning under the curse of sin:

> The creation waits with eager longing for the revealing of the sons of God. For the creation was subjected to futility, not willingly, but because of him who subjected it, in hope that the creation itself will be set free from its bondage to corruption and obtain the freedom of the glory of the children of God. For we know that the whole creation has been groaning together in the pains of childbirth until now. (Rom. 8:19–22)

Paul describes creation as having within it the desire to function according to its original design. Even creation has been impeded by sin from displaying God's glory, as it once did.

In Genesis 3:17–19, we learn a few things about man's relationship to the earth after the fall. It had become cursed. Man was told that it will take pain and sweat equity to get earth to yield its harvest, and there will be thorns and thistles. There is no way for us to know how a pre-cursed garden looked or functioned, but it was surely a paradise. It is hard to imagine what fruits or vegetables would taste like in an un-cursed state. It is hard to imagine the beauty of a sunset or the thrill of animals in the wild, neither afraid nor a threat. Creation still offers humans a glimpse into the glory of God, but it has been radically defaced by the graffiti of sin.

Mission

As God's Glory

God's mission, then, is writing his story through what he treasures. Since his glory is precious to him, his story centers on the declaration of his glory. His glory is reflected in his story through the very unfolding of the story as he is disclosed for who he is and what he does. God is on mission to declare his glory as gracious redeemer and sovereign ruler. The heavy (*kabod*) excellence (*doxa*) of God sets him apart from all:

- Other gods and idols (Isaiah 46; Acts 17:22–31)
- Rulers and powers (Colossians 1; Hebrews 1; 1 Pet. 3:21–22)
- Experiences and pleasures (1 Cor. 2:9; Eph. 3:14–18)

It is God on mission that allows us to comprehend the good things he has prepared for us. It is God on mission when we experience his grace. It is God on mission when we are agents of grace in the life of someone else. It is God on mission when his glory is discerned or displayed. Therefore, when we function according to our design as image bearers, we are in essence joining God on his mission by declaring, displaying, and discerning the glory of God. We are invited to join God on the mission of declaring his glory as image bearers, worshipers, and the people of God, and as those who bear witness to his transforming work in us by bearing his fruit of righteousness (John 15:1–8; Acts 1:8; Heb. 12:7–11).

As the People of God

I am discouraged time and time again when I hear people excuse themselves from engaging culture and getting involved in the lives of those outside the church but stay only inside their spheres of influence in the name of "community." The sticking point for most people seems to be this perception: "We have to choose whether we will be a group that goes deep with one another or one that stays shallow so others can join in at any time." Think back to Acts 2:42–47, which we considered earlier. The early church was involved in the apostles' teaching, fellowship, breaking bread, and prayers (v. 42). They were characterized as souls gripped with awe (v. 43), having all things in common (v. 44), and selling their possessions to distribute the proceeds to all as each had need (v. 45). Have you ever been in a community that was deeper than that? I can't imagine any present-day community more involved in the lives of others, or more transparent and loving, and in the midst of such deep and rich community, the Lord added to their number daily those who were being saved (v. 47).

A community will not remain shallow if its overarching objective is to integrate new people. There is no conflict between authentic community and mission. The people of God involved in one another's lives and working redemptively in the lives of outsiders is the essence of biblical community and biblical mission. As Christopher Wright explains:

> God's new people in Christ are also a people for the sake of the world, and this is to be reflected in their lives. In short, as God's covenant people, Christians are meant to be
>
> • A people who are light to the world by their good lives (1 Peter)
> • A people who are learning obedience and teaching it to the nations (Matthew)
> • A people who love one another in order to show who they belong to (John).[7]

At Mars Hill, we've had several community groups that have helped their members to help their neighbors. We've seen decks built for single moms, houses painted for the elderly, meals brought to pregnant women, and sick and mourning families cared for, even though they are not part of any community. Those in these communities are on mission together to help their members be the hands and heart of Christ to a neighbor. If people are going to dismantle idols and recalibrate worship from self to Jesus, they are going to have to see others doing it to be convinced of its reality and benefits.

It is of no little consequence that Paul calls gathered believers the temple of the Holy Spirit (1 Cor. 3:16). And Jesus says, "You are the salt of the earth, but if salt has lost its taste, how shall its saltiness be restored? It is no longer good for anything except to be thrown out and trampled under people's feet. You are the light of the world. A city set on a hill cannot be hidden" (Matt. 5:13–14). Jesus says that those who follow him are as salt to the earth, and in this context it has to do with enhanced flavor. The people of God are to live to show that life is more savory or tasteful when following Jesus. I don't know too many non-Christians who view Christians as life's savor. Many people when considering Christianity wrestle with giving up what they think is the savor of life to follow Jesus. What a confident claim Jesus makes to those who would follow him. He is essentially saying, "You are giving up less to get more in following me." The more isn't more of the same bland life, but it is actually what gives life its robust flavor.

He goes on to say that his people are the light of the world and not to be hidden. This sounds opposed to the conviction that "we can't be deep and open as a group." Jesus is saying that you can't be deep without also being open, for if you are the light of the world but hide your light, the world remains unlit, which means we contribute to the world's darkness. In short, the only way the people of God can truly be the people of God is by being on mission with God.

Jesus condemned the isolated, religious living of his day. He called the religious leaders "whitewashed tombs" and "hypocrites" for trying to appear life-giving, while on the inside they were decaying (Matt. 23:27). The people of God function as a collective image bearer, showing what grace, truth, love, and transformation look like. These words sound great, but the truth is that the process is often messy, and it is Jesus's greatness in the midst of our mess that calls people out of their own story and into God's. Look at how Jesus restored Peter:

> When they had finished breakfast, Jesus said to Simon Peter, "Simon, son of John, do you love me more than these?" He said to him, "Yes, Lord; you know that I love you." He said to him, "Feed my lambs." He said to him a second time, "Simon, son of John, do you love me?" He said to him, "Yes, Lord; you know that I love you." He said to him, "Tend my sheep." He said to him the third time, "Simon, son of John, do you love me?" Peter was grieved because he said to him the third time, "Do you love me?" and he said to him, "Lord, you know everything; you know that I love you." Jesus said to him, "Feed my sheep. Truly, truly, I say to you, when you were young, you used to dress yourself and walk wherever you wanted, but when you are old, you will stretch out your hands, and another will dress you and carry you where you do not want to go." (This he said to show by what kind of death he was to glorify God.) And after saying this he said to him, "Follow me." (John 21:15–19)

After Peter had denied Jesus three times, Jesus asked him three times whether Peter loved him. The third time Peter was hurt, perhaps because it was a reminder of his three denials, or perhaps it was simply the repeated questioning by Jesus. This, however, is not the author's main point. His main point was to record Jesus's call of Peter. Jesus called Peter to feed his sheep and then explained the death Peter was going to experience.

Jesus is clear that loving him and following him will always have implications. The implication of Peter's loving Jesus was to feed Jesus's disciples and to follow him even to death. Peter was used by the Holy Spirit in a profound way, preaching a spontaneous sermon that jump-started the church with over three thousand converts. This was the fruit of a man following Jesus, with a community of believers (Acts 1:15). God does not deposit his light in the heart of men to be hidden; God does not transform the lives of his children that they would be tasteless in the world in which they live. God's desire is for the very people who delight him to be his instruments in calling others to himself so that others might join him in his story on mission as the people of God.

As Reconciliation

Paul describes Christians' mission as being God's ambassadors:

> Therefore, if anyone is in Christ, he is a new creation. The old has passed away; behold, the new has come. All this is from God, who through Christ reconciled us to himself and gave us the ministry of reconciliation; that is, in Christ God was reconciling the world to himself, not counting their trespasses against them, and entrusting to us the message of reconciliation. Therefore, we are ambassadors for Christ, God making his appeal through us. We implore you on behalf of Christ, be reconciled to God. For our sake he made him to be sin who knew no sin, so that in him we might become the righteousness of God. (2 Cor. 5:17–21)

As you read Paul's words, it is easy to see that the work God intends to do is one of reconciliation, bringing peace between the rebels of the kingdom and the sovereign King. This reconciliation involves more than just a quick spiritual pivot of conversion. This reconciliation is the pervasive gospel message of a redeeming God from beginning to completion.

A good ambassador embodies the country he represents. As ambassadors of Christ we are to embody Jesus and his kingdom. Since, for example, the Trinity delights in creation, an ambassador stewards creation to the pleasure of God. Since the Trinity delights in the people of God, an ambassador of the Trinity loves, serves, and protects the body of Christ. If God is pleased to bring light and life to the world through his people, then a good ambassador is someone who engages his culture so as to bring light and life to the culture and the context in which he lives. We must learn to engage our culture as ambassadors. An ambassador learns to live within the context of a culture, knowing what dimensions of the culture are helpful to adopt, whether that be language, dress, music, or cuisine.

Jesus prayed that his disciples would be protected as they engaged their culture: "I do not ask that you take them out of the world, but that you keep them from the evil one. They are not of the world, just as I am not of the world. Sanctify them in the truth; your word is truth. As you sent me into the world, so I have sent them into the world. And for their sake I consecrate myself, that they also may be sanctified in truth" (John 17:15–19). When he prayed that they would not be taken out of the world, he was praying that they would learn to live in the midst of a dangerous environment. He was confident in the power of God that his disciples would not be infected by the world but be its contagions. They were to become dangerous to the worldliness of the culture by living as salt and light. Jesus's followers did just that. They are described in Acts 17:6 as those who had "turned the world upside down." He prayed that they would be kept from the Evil One. There is an enemy of our soul who desires to destroy our walk with Jesus (1 Pet. 5:8), and it is the very works of the Devil that Jesus came to destroy (1 John 3:8).

There are ways in which we are expected to engage culture as Jesus did. He went to parties and weddings, he observed religious festivals, and he took on the profession of his father. Mark Driscoll describes the various ways a Christian can engage culture as "receiving," "rejecting," or "redeeming." When we receive, it means we share in aspects of our culture, and God's glory is not compromised. There are aspects of a culture, however, that are sheer works of the Devil, and they must be rejected for God to be glorified. Receiving and rejecting are easier to understand than the third category, which is engaging culture in a redemptive way. It is taking something from culture and transforming it with the story of God. For example, social justice has often been a cry of culture. Taking up the cause of the oppressed and bringing a sense of belonging is a way to share in aspects of culture—the receiving category— without compromising the glory of God.

Sometime the issue is more about perspective than behavior. Many churches call their work "mercy ministry" rather than "social justice." *Justice* implies that we have a right to something, whereas mercy implies grace whether deserved or not. The people of God expressing the grace and mercy of God declare the glory of God and, in so reflecting God and his kingdom, they become ambassadors of reconciliation. Whether it is helping the poor, the orphaned, the stranger or alien, or the mentally and physically impaired, extending mercy is declaring the glory of God. Jesus said it this way:

> When the Son of Man comes in his glory, and all the angels with him, then he will sit on his glorious throne. Before him will be gathered all the nations, and he will separate people one from another as a shepherd separates the sheep from the goats. And he will place the sheep on his right, but the goats on the left. Then the King will say to those on his right, "Come, you who are blessed by my Father, inherit the kingdom prepared for you from the foundation of the world. For I was hungry and you gave me food, I was thirsty and you gave me drink, I was a stranger and you welcomed me, I was naked and you clothed me, I was sick and you visited me, I was in prison and you came to me." Then the righteous will answer him, saying, "Lord, when did we see you hungry and feed you, or thirsty and give you drink? And when did we see you a stranger and welcome you, or naked and clothe you? And when did we see you sick or in prison and visit you?" And the King will answer them, "Truly, I say to you, as you did it to one of the least of these my brothers, you did it to me." Then he will say to those on his left, "Depart from me, you cursed, into the eternal fire prepared for the devil and his angels. For

I was hungry and you gave me no food, I was thirsty and you gave me no drink, I was a stranger and you did not welcome me, naked and you did not clothe me, sick and in prison and you did not visit me." Then they also will answer, saying, "Lord, when did we see you hungry or thirsty or a stranger or naked or sick or in prison, and did not minister to you?" Then he will answer them, saying, "Truly, I say to you, as you did not do it to one of the least of these, you did not do it to me." And these will go away into eternal punishment, but the righteous into eternal life. (Matt. 25:31–46)

Jesus is not saying that our acts of mercy are what save us, but he is saying that if we do not image him, we have little cause to believe we are saved. All God's creation, including people, are to experience the fruit of God's redeeming us. Our presence is to be a redemptive presence in our culture. It is to ruin darkness with light; it is to enhance our culture as salt or seasoning. Our compelling missional thought should be to so embed ourselves in what is right about our culture that people would weep if we as the people of God were removed from it.

Even though Jesus warns us that we should not expect to be thought of or treated better than or different from how the world treated him:

If the world hates you, know that it has hated me before it hated you. If you were of the world, the world would love you as its own; but because you are not of the world, but I chose you out of the world, therefore the world hates you. Remember the word that I said to you: "A servant is not greater than his master." If they persecuted me, they will also persecute you. If they kept my word, they will also keep yours. But all these things they will do to you on account of my name, because they do not know him who sent me. (John 15:18–21)

Jesus was executed for fear that he might draw a following: "So the chief priests and the Pharisees gathered the Council and said, "What are we to do? For this man performs many signs. If we let him go on like this, everyone will believe in him'" (John 11:47–48). And yet, his following grew exponentially. Mission has the sweet byproduct of seeing people come to Jesus and become part of the people of God. To be on mission with God is to respond to the high calling to participate with him on his mission in his story.

CHAPTER 9 ASSIGNMENT

Read Stephen's speech (Acts 7). Take time to journal and pray through this passage on the spread of the gospel.

Engaging Missional Thinking

1) Read Genesis 3:14–19. How extensive is the ruin caused by sin?
2) Read Psalm 31. Contrast living in the fallen world with hoping in the Lord.
3) Read Matthew 16:13–20. How does Jesus portray the matchup between the church and the gates of hell? How would you relate this to the church's mission?
4) How does Stephen engage his audience's culture with the gospel (Acts 7)?
5) Read Acts 26:1–29. How does Paul use his story and citizenship as a platform for mission?

Digging Deeper

Use the following verses to sensitize you to God's heart for mission. Record your convictions and action points.

2 Kings 17:25–28
1 Chronicles 16:23–24
Psalm 18:49
Psalm 96:2–5
Isaiah 43:6–7
Daniel 4:28–37
Jonah 3:1–10
Matthew 24:14
Matthew 28:19
Mark 16:15–16
Luke 9:1–6
Luke 10:1–24
Luke 13:28–30
Luke 14:23–24

Luke 24:44–49
Acts 1:1–11
Acts 2:1–41
Acts 8:4–40
Acts 9:1–31
Acts 10–11
Acts 13:2–5
Acts 13:47
1 Corinthians 16:9
Revelation 14:6–7

10

MISSION DISTORTIONS

I was having coffee with a friend, when she paused in the conversation and asked me, "Bill, can I ask you something without you thinking I'm stupid?" I told her that I didn't think I could promise that up front, and after that weak attempt at putting her at ease, I pledged safety that she could ask me whatever she was thinking. She then said, "What does *missional* mean? It just sounds like a made-up word." I said, "Well, every word is actually a made-up word." Her question was really profound, however, because the word *missional* has come to mean so many different things. When people join God on his mission, they have become missional. This perspective gets to the heart of what I mean when I talk about calling people to mission. Attempting to understand the meaning of *mission* seems to set up distortions of one kind or another.

The "Only" Distortions

It is easy to make the one thing you do, or the one thing you're missing, be the ingredient that truly defines mission. For many, the only thing necessary is a message. Let's call this "evangelism." Are there really Christian people against evangelism as the proclamation of the message of Jesus Christ? This is also a hard question to answer. There are relatively few Christians who would object to proclaiming Jesus as the Son of God who came to earth as a man, died on a cross, and rose from the dead. The problem begins when Christians believe the mission is complete as soon as these basic truths have been proclaimed. Listen to Jesus's own words:

> Then the King will say to those on his right, "Come, you who are blessed by my Father, inherit the kingdom prepared for you from the foundation of the world. For I was hungry and you gave me food, I was thirsty and you gave me drink, I was a stranger and you welcomed me, I was naked and you clothed me, I was sick and you visited me, I was in prison and you came to me." Then the righteous will answer him, saying, "Lord, when did we see you hungry and feed you, or thirsty and give you drink? And when did we see you a stranger and welcome you, or naked and clothe you? And when did we see you sick or in prison and visit you?" And the King will answer them, "Truly, I say to you, as you did it to one of the least of these my brothers, you did it to me." (Matt. 25:34–40)

We can make two observations from those verses. (1) Jesus depicts a scene in which people are going to be rewarded by the King for how they have served him. Jesus points to those who have served their King well. They are those who have expressed value and worth to the marginalized of the world by meeting their needs and treating them with dignity. (2) The King identifies with the marginalized of the world and tells his listeners that those who would be rewarded in the coming kingdom will be those who demonstrate mercy and love, granting dignity to the outcasts of the world. Jesus definitely puts a pin into the balloon of mission as evangelism only. The kingdom Jesus brings is one of eternal life. For this to mean anything, it must mean that life is qualitatively different, not merely longer.

The second "only" distortion is that evangelism is mercy only. Several Christian leaders have influenced me to use the word *mercy* rather than *social justice*, since, as we noted earlier, social justice implies getting what we deserve. The bad news is that we all deserve the wrath of God, so to opt for mercy is to extend the very grace we have received. In the Sermon on the Mount, Jesus makes the appeal to his listeners to be righteous toward enemies, not just to those in the Christian community. Jesus's rationale for such a demand was the profile of the heavenly Father: "For he makes his sun rise on the evil and on the good, and sends rain on the just and on the unjust" (Matt. 5:45). Again, Jesus ties the kingdom of God to the God of the kingdom; as members of God's kingdom, we must see ourselves as disclosers of God's mysteries by the very way we live out his kingdom on this planet. Paul, however, suggests that without the declaring of the gospel, people may not be able to connect the dots between a truth displayed and the need for a truth to be applied (Rom. 10:17). We must be both displays of the kingdom and declarations of the kingdom by King-drenched actions and words.[1]

The "only" distortions go even further with behavior-modification views of transformation and helping. In the name of mission, many people establish programs aimed at transforming negative or sinful character traits. While I welcome eliminating enslaving, destructive habits from people's lives, freedom from enslaving habits is not the gospel. It's not the behavior only that needs to be cast off; rather, it's what is in the heart. The distortion comes in because those freed from habitual sin take on that freedom as their new identity; however, the gospel is about identity transfer, not identity improvement: "I have been crucified with Christ. It is no longer I who live, but Christ who lives in me. And the life I now live in the flesh I live by faith in the Son of God, who loved me and gave himself for me" (Gal. 2:20).

A missional program of transformation will deal with the personal and cultural idols that set themselves up in the place of Jesus: "For though we walk in the flesh, we are not waging war according to the flesh. For the weapons of our warfare are not of the flesh but have divine power to destroy strongholds. We destroy arguments and every lofty opinion raised against the knowledge of God, and take every thought captive to obey Christ" (2 Cor. 10:3–5). A person on mission will help others step away from the shadows, and behavior will definitely change. However, it will not be the benchmark of transformation, nor can it be the only aspect of the effort labeled "mission."

Another distortion of mission is apologetics. Recently I was on a consulting call, and a young man in training for the ministry shared with me a concern about his theological training. He had been noticing a shift away from talking about Jesus toward debating theology. I have to admit that I am somewhat attracted to the Irish pub phrase "Is this a private fight, or can anybody join in?" I like the feelings and the growth that happen as we stretch each other's thinking and bring perspectives to bear on the one- or two-dimensional blind spots inherent in individualism.

Apologetics, however, at best is a partner with evangelism and it has the same charges leveled against it. Apologists do the hard work of contextualizing arguments and dealing with the issues raised by culture. In arguments, however, they must demonstrate compassion toward those they hope to convince of the existence of a loving, transforming God. When defending the faith trumps embodying the faith, the gospel seems indefensible.

Chart 10.1: Mission's Heart

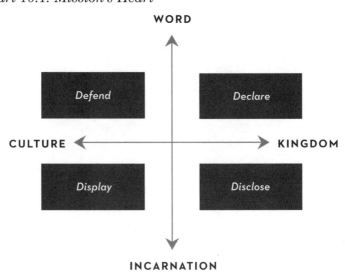

Often those who gravitate toward a gospel of defense are those with strong prophetic inclinations for declaring truth without the mercy concerns for the damage or wounds caused by how the truth was delivered. A truly Spirit-filled apologist realizes that most arguments constructed against the gospel require points of care and compassion for the subjective as much as points of logic and reason for the objective.

Developing a Heart for Mission

Based on chart 10.1, let's look at a few of the tensions that shape a heart for mission.

Declare

The discipline of declaring the gospel is counterintuitive. The gospel is a message of love and hope, but it also causes offense because of its exclusive claims.

> You hypocrites! Well did Isaiah prophesy of you, when he said: "This people honors me with their lips, but their heart is far from me; in vain do they worship me, teaching as doctrines the commandments of men." And he called the people to him and said to them, "Hear and understand: it is not what goes into the mouth that defiles a person, but what comes out of the mouth; this defiles a person." Then the disciples came and said to him, "Do you know that the Pharisees were offended when they heard this saying?" He answered, "Every plant that my heavenly Father has not planted will be rooted up. Let them alone; they are blind guides. And if the blind lead the blind, both will fall into a pit." (Matt. 15:7–14)
>
> For the word of the cross is folly to those who are perishing, but to us who are being saved it is the power of God. For it is written, "I will destroy the wisdom of the wise, and the discernment of the discerning I will thwart." Where is the one who is wise? Where is the scribe? Where is the debater of this age? Has not God made foolish the wisdom of the world? For since, in the wisdom of God, the world did not know God through

wisdom, it pleased God through the folly of what we preach to save those who believe. For Jews demand signs and Greeks seek wisdom, but we preach Christ crucified, a stumbling block to Jews and folly to Gentiles, but to those who are called, both Jews and Greeks, Christ the power of God and the wisdom of God. For the foolishness of God is wiser than men, and the weakness of God is stronger than men. (1 Cor. 1:18–25)

So, whether you eat or drink, or whatever you do, do all to the glory of God. Give no offense to Jews or to Greeks or to the church of God, just as I try to please everyone in everything I do, not seeking my own advantage, but that of many, that they may be saved. (1 Cor. 10:31–33)

These passages show us that Jesus's teachings offended religious leaders. We also see Paul observing that the gospel, with its crucified Savior, was culturally offensive to Jews. Greeks too took offense at a resurrected Savior. Taken together, we can conclude from these passages that it is nothing short of a supernatural work of God breaking into a person's heart that explains the kingdom phenomenon of mission.

Disclose

To *disclose* suggests something is hidden or needs to be revealed. In Jesus's priestly prayer, he asks that his disciples' love for one another may reveal his true identity to the world:

> *[handwritten: make holy, sanctify, set apart for service—to perform the Father's wishes Cross]*
> As you sent me into the world, so I have sent them into the world. And for their sake I consecrate myself, that they also may be sanctified in truth. I do not ask for these only, but also for those who will believe in me through their word, that they may all be one, just as you, Father, are in me, and I in you, that they also may be in us, so that the world may believe that you have sent me. (John 17:18–21)

Jesus was sending his disciples into the world as the Father had sent him. Here is bedrock truth for the conviction of mission and that we are joining a sending God on his mission as sent ones.

Jesus envisioned the power of believers living out the gospel would itself be convincing proof that Jesus had been sent from the Father as the redeemer of man's soul. Part of mission, then, is disclosing the invisible kingdom through visible means. We are conduits of God's grace to a sin-stained world.

> All human beings are made in God's image, and as a result there are many implications for our mission arising from the common humanity that we share with all other inhabitants of our planet. And yet all people are also radically and comprehensively infected and affected by sin and evil. Our missional response must be as radical and comprehensive as the problem we address in the name of Christ and the power of the cross.[2]

People catch a glimpse of the King through subjects who live according to his rule. As forgiven and forgiving, as loved and loving, and as in-covenant and keeping-covenant people, we essentially put God on display to the world:

> But we have renounced disgraceful, underhanded ways. We refuse to practice cunning or to tamper with God's word, but by the open statement of the truth we would commend ourselves to everyone's conscience in the sight of God. And even if our gospel is veiled, it is veiled only to those who are perishing. In their case the god of this world has blinded the minds of the unbelievers, to keep them from seeing the light of the gospel of the glory of Christ, who is the image of God. For what we proclaim is not ourselves, but Jesus Christ as Lord, with ourselves as your servants for Jesus' sake. For God, who said, "Let light shine out of darkness," has shone in our hearts to give the light of the knowledge of the glory of God in the face of Jesus Christ. (2 Cor. 4:2–6)

Paul tells the Corinthians that (1) the gospel is veiled to those who are perishing; (2) the god of this world (Satan) blinds unbelievers to the gospel; and (3) the best way we can participate with God in shining light into darkness is to renounce disgraceful and underhanded practices and to live lives consistent with our King and his kingdom. This means that we disclose the gospel and participate with God on his mission by being people of transforming character.

Display

Rather than hiding the gospel in our personal lifestyle and choices, we seek to display the good news of Jesus and his kingdom in tangible means within the context of the unbelieving world in which we live. Those who do not know the gospel benefit from those who do know it. Hungry people are fed, homeless people are sheltered, sick people are attended to, and the love goes on.

I have had the privilege of working with several men from the Union Gospel Mission in Seattle. Together we have opened up nonalcoholic stage shows, a restaurant, and a coffeehouse and have provided classes, and some of our people have provided housing and employment for men as they transitioned out of recovery residential care. Several of the men expressed feeling overwhelmed and shocked that they were treated as normal human beings.

One of the men approached me at a Christmas party at my house and said, "Bill, I don't know what to do. I have never been at a party where we weren't getting loaded." He was learning how to have fun without next-morning regrets. Another man was surprised when I picked him up from the mission and asked him what he wanted to do. He figured I would give him a hot meal and then just drop him off at the mission again. That afternoon we did have a hot meal, but he wanted to play eighteen holes of golf, so we did. We spent the afternoon as peers. Another man wanted to volunteer on Friday nights, cooking and busing tables at our church coffeehouse. After a couple of months, we changed the menu to offer some of the dishes he enjoyed making.

These men and others were in a community group with me for over two years. We ate and recreated together. I didn't see them as projects or as guys from the mission. They were image bearers, and I learned as much about God and myself from them as I have from any of my other friends.

Of course, there were frustrations during and after this time. Some of the men proved to be bad employees so that others were hesitant to hire any of the men. Others were hesitant to offer friendship for fear they would be used and abandoned. Some men were avoided altogether.

Displaying the kingdom can be as simple as doing benevolent acts, but acts alone lack the ability to offer dignity in the process. Relationships are the Velcro strips that allow benevolent acts to stick as kingdom deeds. When we infuse our kind acts with real relationships, we correct the distortion that mission is simply social justice, and it becomes reconciliation.

Defend

"In your hearts honor Christ the Lord as holy, always being prepared to make a defense to anyone who asks you for a reason for the hope that is in you; yet do it with gentleness and respect" (1 Pet. 3:15). This verse is a favorite of apologists because it talks about being ready to defend your hope with a rationale. Some people forget to see that the trigger to a discussion of the gospel is someone's asking about it. In the context of this verse, it is the believer who is suffering without complaint who gets asked about his faith. Enduring suffering well and being questioned can't be scheduled in a two-day planner. Many just arm themselves with a defense for their faith whether or not they are asked for it, which feels about like inviting yourself to a neighbor's house for dinner because you want to change your neighbor's eating habits. Unfortunately, most defenses of the faith lead with an attempt to convert someone of another faith to Christ without building the friendship that can bear the weight of heavy questions and truth.

Let's reframe *defend* in terms of living missionally. How does the opportunity for a defense of your hope arise? You or someone you know experiences a crisis and then the question arises: "Why did God let this happen?" or, "How can you believe in a God that would let this happen?" At this point, the rehearsed or researched answers just come across as too polished; unbelievers questioning the nature of God want to hear what is fermenting in your soul, not lines you have memorized. So it is at this moment the gospel and the kingdom of God are subjected to the volatile context of life for their articulation. This is what it means to be on mission with God. It was when Jesus wept that they believed he loved Lazarus (John 11:35). It was when he calmed a storm in the midst of the disciples' terror that they worshiped him as God (Luke 8:22–25). It was at midnight when cells opened and life was at risk that a jailer asked Paul, "What must I do to be saved?" (Acts 16:25–40).

Defending the gospel has way more to do with why you believe than why someone else should believe. As the authors of *Total Church* say, "Apologetics is answering the questions raised by our lives."[3] Your defense of the gospel is more about God's story of redeeming love and how that love redeemed you. Think about the Bible for a few minutes. How much of the Bible is abstract, and how much of it is biography? I am thinking the vast majority of it is biography. Even when we look at Paul's writing, we are not looking at manuscripts submitted to a publisher with a view toward a wide and timeless readership; rather, we are reading letters written to relatively small churches or geographical clusters of churches that are struggling with concrete issues.

Mission should include being able to address the damaging caricatures of Jesus, the church, and what it is to become a Christian. Mission should include the identification of a culture's idols as well as contextualizing the gospel message by constructing bridges of trust and deconstructing the barriers of mistrust.

Hopefully you recognize the great distortions that have occurred in attempts to defend the faith. In past decades it has been more about defaming people and positions than about faming Jesus and his kingdom. The religious crowd meant to slander Jesus when they called him "a friend of . . . sinners" (Luke 7:34). Certainly Jesus was a master at defending the gospel, yet we see him doing it by parable (drawing a parallel circumstance or analogy that poses a puzzle that requires faith to solve it), by paradigm (embodying the very truths and values he proclaimed, as in the example of not condemning the woman caught in adultery, John 7:53–8:11), and by paradox (taking the very contradiction to a conclusion and calling for faith in his hearer to reconcile the tension, Mark 10:23–31).

Jesus's sharpest rebukes were reserved for those who claimed to be followers of the true and living God but were not. He fiercely defended the truth by attacking the distortions being promoted by a religiously lost crowd. The religious community of Jesus's day had made their own Tower of Babel; they believed they could access God on their own terms through deed and ritual. This is where we see Jesus fighting to inject truth regarding righteousness and faith. Jesus's harshest words were toward those who claimed to be the gatekeepers to the kingdom that Jesus was announcing. It was incongruous for the King to be disregarded, in fact, executed, by kingdom members. Only one message could prevail.

In our defense of the gospel, it would be good for us to reflect on the tone of our mission. There is a place for anger and a place for defaming, but it should be reserved for those who claim the kingdom while denying the King. For the rest, the defensive mode of mission is way more about letting Jesus be seen as the hope and hero of the gospel and his kingdom.

To live in only one quadrant of chart 10.1 is to live only one aspect of mission, and it will bring each of us to a ceiling in our mission as disciples. If we can see ourselves as seeking a radical middle where all aspects of mission converge in our life and lifestyle and relating to our neighbors outside the community of faith, we will find ourselves following Jesus in a way that joyfully joins him on mission for his glory.

CHAPTER 10 ASSIGNMENT

Exploring Mission and Its Distortions

1) Read Exodus 33:14–16. What did Moses see as the impact of a people experiencing the presence of God?

2) Read Daniel 9:3–19. What sins does Daniel confess? What do you make of Daniel's confessing, "We have not listened to your . . . prophets" (v. 6)? How does this prayer address missional distortions?

3) Read Acts 18:1–17. How did having a ministry team help Paul in Corinth? How does verse 10 encourage you to see your city through missional eyes?

4) Read Colossians 4:2–6. What does Paul ask the Colossians to pray for him? How does Paul describe missional living in these verses?

5) Read 1 Timothy 3:2–7 and Titus 1:7–9. What qualifications for church leaders have impact on the church's mission? Why do you think missional living matters to God as a qualification for leading the church?

Exploring Mission

As you look at the passages below on renewal and repentance, make note of how our walk with God and our witness of God are tied together.

Old Testament Renewal[4]

Genesis 35:1–15

1 Samuel 7:1–13

1 Kings 18

2 Chronicles 14–16

2 Chronicles 20

2 Chronicles 30:1–9

2 Chronicles 34–35

Haggai 1; Zechariah 1:1–6

Nehemiah 8

Old Testament Repentance

Leviticus 26:40–42

Numbers 21:7

Deuteronomy 4:29–31

Deuteronomy 30:1–10; 32:29

2 Samuel 24:10, 17

1 Kings 8:33–50

2 Chronicles 7:14

2 Chronicles 29:6

2 Chronicles 30:6–9

Ezra 9:4–14

Nehemiah 1:6–9

Nehemiah 9:33–35

Job 7:20; 9:20

Job 33:26–32

Job 34:31–32; 36:10; 40:4; 42:5

Psalm 22:27

Psalm 32:5

Psalm 34:14–18

Psalm 51

Isaiah 6:5

11

PLAN

Discipleship by now may sound as busy and frantic as twelve days of Christmas with leaping lords, swimming swans, and geese a-laying. In this chapter we're going to consider what a disciple's life looks like in daily and weekly slices. Let's start by recapping a sense of identity as a disciple of Jesus. God works his grace gift of salvation by remaking us into his image through Jesus, our new Adam. In response to God, we image back to him his excellence and our praise; this is our sacrifice of joy (Heb. 12:28–29; 13:15), which is worship due to the triune God of the universe. As worshiping image bearers share life together, God's grace is experienced and expressed in the oneness of community. This community is composed of ambassadors for Christ who carry the inviting message, "Be reconciled to God." This puts us smack in the middle of God's story, joining him on mission.

That sounds like a changed life to me. This chapter is about taking the life-changing truths regarding discipleship and putting them into a plan for a changed life. When you think about all that we have covered: imaging and worshiping God as a lifestyle and living in community on mission, you probably think (1) "I can't do this!" (2) "I can do this!" or (3) "How do I do this?" All three are healthy responses. The truth is that apart from the gracious work of God in your life, you can't do this. It is equally true, however, that because of the redemptive work of Jesus and empowering work of the Holy Spirit, you can do this. So, let's take some time to think through how one lives this life of following Jesus.

If you responded, "I can't do this," perhaps you have a sticking point. Below is a short list of discipleship hurdles.

Hurdles

1) Habitual Sin

Habitual sins are ungodly strongholds that you have constructed during your life's journey. These include actions and attitudes of commission (participation) as well as omission (avoidance or neglect). There are patterns in most of our lives that manifest out of unresolved issues and unidentified idols. We do well to take a personal inventory of any such sticking points, but a loving and transformational community can serve us well in identifying where our deceptive hearts are dull to perceive.

2) A Debilitating Mindset

There are numerous things that can sabotage our discipleship. A fearful mind-set is one. Earlier we looked at what Scripture calls "the fear of man" (Prov. 29:25). When we are caught in the fear of man, we are allowing ourselves to be shaped by what people think of us rather than by what God thinks.

Personal failures can also cripple our mind-set. Past failure can distort our present identity, and the risk of failing again can trump the reward of succeeding. When we take on the false identity of "I am my failure," we are not free to pursue our true identity: "I have been called to image God."

Wounds brought on us by others can warp our thinking also. However, if we hang on to such offenses, we become a virtual kaleidoscope of distortions to imaging God's light. We may think we are damaged beyond repair because of things that have happened to us, but the Bible actually tells us that God's strength is seen through our weaknesses: "'My grace is sufficient for you, for my power is made perfect in weakness.' Therefore I will boast all the more gladly of my weaknesses, so that the power of Christ may rest upon me" (2 Cor. 12:9). No matter the origin of our wounds, we cannot be damaged beyond God's ability to heal.

A warped mind-set also springs from seeing ourselves as victims. Today's current forms of psychological healing seek to banish guilt by annihilating personal responsibility. There certainly are cases in which a sufferer's problems are the fault of others, but there is a tremendous difference between acknowledging wrongs done to us and using those wrongs to shape our identity. Staying stuck as a victim is a "stay in jail free" card. It becomes a way for us to stay off the hook for the life we are living. "It's not my fault," we say. "If I had what they've got, I'd be different." While serving as a television commentator for *Monday Night Football*, "Dandy" Don Meredith used to say, "If if's and buts were candy and nuts, we'd all have a merry Christmas." In his own style he was saying that we don't get to live in the world of "what ifs" because we live in the world of what is. Don't let what has happened to you keep you from experiencing what has happened for you through the death and resurrection of Jesus.

A debilitated mind can also come from being uninformed. I have heard it said that "ignorance of the law is no excuse," meaning that not knowing any better is not a criminal defense. It may be true that you just don't know what to do, but staying ignorant is staying stuck. There is more information available to us as Christians today than at any other time in the history of the church. Study Bibles, sermons on the Web, books, studies, and study tools abound. Developing a plan to expose yourself to Jesus and his teaching is part of what it means to be a disciple. Each of us must own the responsibility to know what it looks like to walk as Jesus did (1 John 2:6).

Our mind-set is also shaped by our relationships, and at times we might find ourselves in relationships that keep us from pursuing Jesus. Some examples from people in my life include a teenager who has trusted Christ but her parents are outraged and dead set against her pursuing her faith; a single mom who has little discretionary time, funds, or energy for spending a night in a community group or for availing herself of Bible study resources; a college guy who is so wrapped up in the friendships of his fraternity house he "loses" as many times as he "wins" at standing for Jesus; and a man whose job takes him on the road weekly, making it "impossible" to establish or maintain Christlike rhythms in his life. While each of these situations is complex, each one can learn to respect authority, honor others, and develop disciplines that will call their heart toward Jesus. We can all fall prey to the lie that if it weren't for our family, our situation, our friends, or our work, we could follow Jesus.

3) Priority Management

For others, it is not relationships or work environment that militates against following Jesus, as much as the fact that they have never developed a perspective of what it means to follow Jesus. Considering our time, finances, family, work, personal passions, and skill set are all part of finding our fit in the community called "the body of Christ." Making time to assess and adjust our lifestyle is a critical discipline in following Jesus. "Mission creep" is a term often used to describe organizations that slowly lose focus on their mission and simply work on ways to be more efficient or productive. The problem with that is obvious: if they are no longer on their mission, they really don't need to be more productive.

I have volunteered at several shelters, including a few in the San Francisco area. One shelter fed about three hundred people a day. Volunteers came in a couple of hours before meal time to prepare the food, then women and children were given about an hour to eat and clear out before the men were invited in. In this way women and children were given a safe environment, while the men were cared for personally and treated with dignity as they were later invited in to their meal. I also served at another shelter across town where over 1,500 meals were served daily. I talked to a few servers and clients and found that many of them were not actually volunteers but were fulfilling their obligation to community service. As a result, the clients often felt like cattle rather than people. It is a great thing to serve 1,500 meals to homeless people, but somewhere along the line, the mission creep from care and dignity to efficiency and numbers began to take place.

Take as long as you need to honestly identify and describe in writing how any of these sticking points can keep or has kept you from following Jesus. If you have experienced sticking points that do not fit in these categories, then include them as well in your list of hurdles to living as Jesus's disciple.

Moving Forward

Now, let's draw upon a few concepts we covered earlier:

1) God is three relational persons, living in community as Trinity.
2) We are to reflect God as image bearers.
3) We must live in community with significant relationships in order to image God accurately.

Because of these truths, any plan we devise for following Jesus must include at least one other disciple. In the next chapter we will look at the notion of discipling others by extending to them a relationship that calls them to image God to you and with you. But for now, let's focus on seeking a disciple-making disciple in your own life. If we were to make a list of what roles this person might play in your life, the options could include:

- A *counselor* to address your emotional sticking points.
- A *coach* to call you to accountability for the goals you set.
- A *pastor* to provide spiritual direction.
- An *encourager* to provide the inspiration to "hang in there" and not give up.
- A *peer* to serve as an influencer.
- A *consultant* to provide information and input.
- An *example* to provide a template through their experience.

- A *mentor* who is a life stage or two ahead of you to provide wisdom.
- A *friend* with whom to walk through the journey.
- A *partner* who labors toward the same cause.

The beauty of such a list of specialists is that each can serve a function or provide a task, a correction, or a direction for your life.

There are, however, a few downsides to discipling relationships as well. First, our lives aren't neatly segmented so as to be spiritually, emotionally, or functionally transformed by such surgically precise strikes. Life seems to defy the formulaic and bleeds from neat categories into a messy mosaic. For this reason, relational connections outweigh functional connections when it comes to transformation and discipleship.

Second, most of us don't have the relational bandwidth to carry around ten intense relationships in which the primary function is that of personal coach or trainer. Image bearers, as we have already seen, develop relationships with others in community and on mission. To now add a whole new cadre of friends to form "team me" is way more a therapeutic and behavioral focus than the transformational impact of disciple making portrayed in Scripture.

The Bible uses a metaphor for transformational leadership—shepherd. Psalm 23 is one of the most familiar psalms and depicts someone being shepherded by the Lord himself. In his book *The Shepherd Leader*, Timothy Witmer identifies four major functions of a shepherd: (1) knowing the sheep, (2) feeding the sheep, (3) leading the sheep, and (4) protecting the sheep.[1] We see all four functions present in Psalm 23:

1) *Knowing.* In verse 3 the shepherd restores the soul; in verse 4 there is a comforting personal presence; and in verse 5 there is a caregiving act of anointing the head with oil.
2) *Feeding.* In verse 2 the one being shepherded is made to lie down in green pastures and brought to still waters, and in verse 5 he has a table set before him.

3) *Leading.* In verse 3 the shepherd leads in paths of righteousness for his name's sake.

4) *Protecting.* In verse 4 there is no fear of evil, and the shepherds rod and staff are a comfort. In verse 5 the table set
before the sheep is in the presence of enemies.

Ezekiel 34 is a treatise on bad shepherding and God's inter-
vening. Look at the following observations:

The bad shepherds of Israel are condemned for feeding on
the sheep instead of feeding the sheep (vv. 2, 8). In verse 16, the
shepherds are condemned for their lack of care. Specifically,
the weak are not strengthened; the sick are not healed; the
injured are not bound up; the straying are not brought back;
and the lost are not sought. Additionally, shepherdless herds
injure one another. They tread down the grass so others cannot graze, and they muddy pristine drinking water (v. 18); and
they push each other aside, thrust the weak with their horns,
and cause one another to be scattered (v. 21). God then says
he will be Israel's shepherd by searching for his sheep (v. 11);
seeking out and rescuing his sheep (vv. 11, 12, 16); bringing
back his sheep (vv. 13, 16); and feeding them with good pasture
(vv. 14–15). God's way of turning this around is by being the
shepherd to his people.

> I will rescue my flock; they shall no longer be a prey. And I will
> judge between sheep and sheep. And I will set up over them one
> shepherd, my servant David, and he shall feed them: he shall
> feed them and be their shepherd. And I, the LORD, will be their
> God, and my servant David shall be prince among them. I am
> the LORD; I have spoken. (vv. 22–24)

Jesus identifies himself with this role in John 10:11 by claiming, "I am the good shepherd. The good shepherd lays down his
life for the sheep." In this one verse Jesus both identifies with
God's plan for his sheep and articulates the heart of shepherding.
Where the condemned shepherds of Ezekiel were self-serving

and sheep destroying, the good shepherd is self-sacrificing and sheep rescuing.

When we pair this with Jesus's commission to his disciples in Matthew 28, to make disciples, we see that Jesus as the shepherd leads people through his people. While we follow Jesus, he does the work of knowing, feeding, leading, and protecting through those who are following him. In the context of the church, elders are called "shepherds." Paul commissioned Timothy as a church leader to disciple men who could disciple men: "And what you have heard from me in the presence of many witnesses entrust to faithful men who will be able to teach others also" (2 Tim. 2:2).

So while the primary task of shepherding or leading the church falls to elders, disciples are expected to shepherd each other as part of what it means to make disciples. Implied through the rebuke in Ezekiel is that a well-shepherded flock contributes to the health of all the sheep. Perhaps the best way to look at the "one anothers" of Scripture and the mandate to make disciples is to think of all having a shepherd-coach in their life who can help them move forward in their call to follow Jesus. Framing your discipleship plan with another person who can function as a shepherd-coach in your life is a huge step in following Jesus.

I find it fascinating that we don't find disciples going it alone in the New Testament. Mark writes, "He called the twelve and began to send them out two by two, and gave them authority over the unclean spirits" (Mark 6:7). And Luke says, "After this the Lord appointed seventy-two others and sent them on ahead of him, two by two, into every town and place where he himself was about to go" (Luke 10:1). Even when the apostle Paul began his missionary career, Barnabas was sent with him (Acts 11:22–30; 13:1–3). And when Paul and Barnabas finally parted ways, they both enlisted other disciples to continue with them on their respective missions (Acts 15:36–41). In Jesus, we see a life full of grace and truth. "For the law was given through Moses; grace and truth came through Jesus Christ" (John 1:17).

Looking at Paul's letter to one of his disciples, Titus, we see a close link between deed (actions or good works) and word (speech and teaching):

> Show yourself in all respects to be a model of good works, and in your teaching show integrity, dignity, and sound speech that cannot be condemned, so that an opponent may be put to shame, having nothing evil to say about us. (Titus 2:7–8; see also 1:6; 2:14; 3:1, 8, 14)

Plotting these coordinates we find somewhat of a shepherding compass:

Chart 11.1: Shepherding Compass

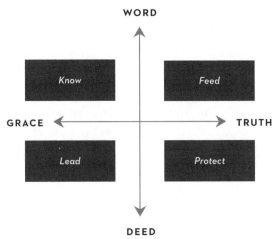

Using these coordinates we can develop a plan for discipleship and shepherding.

Quadrant 1: Grace + Word = Knowing

The relational dynamic of shepherd and sheep communicating suggests sheep that are known and a shepherd that is being known and followed (John 10:3–4). You as a disciple must be willing to both disclose and communicate. Disclosing your sticking points or hurdles to following Jesus and communicating your picture of what life looks like pursuing Jesus will involve your relationships, affections, and thoughts.

The role of a shepherd in knowing you and in developing a loving transformational relationship with you includes spending time with you and asking questions, not just as a fact-finding mission but for the purpose of opening up communication and trust. While communication is being established and deepened, the shepherd must discipline himself or herself to be a good listener. There will be a time to inform, clarify, or correct, but in getting to know the disciple, the shepherd has a primary responsibility to listen for attitudes of the heart. If a disciple feels that he is just one more disciple, dismissed or "clichéd," chances are that the shepherding is springing more from a template than from a relationship.

My wife is not much of a sushi fan. When she humors me and we go to a sushi bar, I will comment on whether I like it, whether I think it is good sushi. Her question to me is, "How can it be good or bad? It's *raw* fish!" This question comes from a failure to see the art of sushi making. There probably isn't much the chef can do to the taste of raw fish and rice; the art of sushi making is in creating the roll with texture. Just so, there is an art to shepherding disciples, to coaching them in the formation of their gospel identity. The distinctive is not so much in the ingredients but in the personal interaction, the influence, and the ability to interact because of knowing the disciple as an individual.

Quadrant 2: Truth + Word = Feeding

In this quadrant the dynamics include learning and feeding. As a disciple you must have a life rhythm of learning. This means you see yourself as a student able to learn from teachers, circumstances, and experiences. As a learner you are committing to a trajectory of drawing closer to all three persons of the Trinity, living a life that images the God who creates, redeems, and matures you.

The role of shepherd as a feeder is to teach the disciple how to observe (live out) the commands of Christ:

> Go therefore and make disciples of all nations, baptizing them in the name of the Father and of the Son and of the Holy Spirit, *teaching them to observe all that I have commanded you.* (Matt. 28:19–20)

This means time in the Word together along with discussions about applications and implications to life. A good shepherd at this point knows how to assign learning projects to the disciple, which can range from a focused study, to disciplines like journaling, to a day of solitude and prayer, to challenging the disciple to frame "what a win looks like" in a reconciled relationship. The bottom line is that most of what it looks like to follow Jesus is caught rather than taught. If you are discipling someone or preparing to, you should schedule a half day of solitude and ask God to help you recall all that you have had to learn to follow Jesus. The likelihood is that those you disciple will have to learn the same things, and God has brought you into their lives because you are the curriculum.

When I was in college, I took the course work to be certified as a social worker. The mantra of our school was "A social worker is as good as his ability to refer." When it comes to discipleship, shepherds must know where to refer their disciples to find good food. Good shepherds will point to a good study Bible such as the ESV; resource websites such as The Resurgence and Desiring God; and biblically sound churches such as Mars Hill, The Journey, The Village, and Imago Dei where they can hear the gospel contextualized on mission in the community of a local church.

When disciples are fed well, they develop a sense of being empowered to serve as lifelong learners. The bad shepherds of Ezekiel 34 were feeding upon the sheep rather than feeding the sheep. When a sheep feels battered rather than bettered, the shepherding has probably not been as much about feeding as about condemnation and motivation by guilt.

Quadrant 3: Grace + Deed = Leading

Let's look first at the disciple's role in this quadrant and then at some shepherd functions that can help lead the disciple. As a disciple, your challenge is to integrate being with doing. For this to happen, it becomes even more critical that you have a picture of what your life looks like when you're following Jesus. Whether you call this a vision, a mission, or a purpose statement is not the point; having a compelling picture that calls you to action is. This means taking the aspects of discipleship and personalizing them as your own.

When you envision imaging God, does it include a picture of your health, things you can do, strengths you have, and the uniqueness of your personality, talents, and gifting? While each of us images God, each of us will image him with our unique signature. God's grace allows you to envision the good works he has prepared for you to do (Eph. 2:8–10). When you envision what it looks like to be a worshiper, does it include your income (not just your giving but all your resources), your time and availability, and what it would mean to live by faith outside of your own ability to manage life? These issues must be part of your picture of a worshiping disciple.

Regarding community, what would it look like to image God through your relationships—friends, family, neighbors, and work acquaintances? As you address the idea of mission, how will you meet and connect with people who have not yet signed on to God's story as their story? Will they be invited into your life as a friend, someone who could help you? Will you share a cause with them? What kind of life rhythms will you develop: weekly meals or classes at a college, community center, or health club? Are you willing to rearrange your life for the sake of living in frequent, personal proximity to non-Christians? What does an ideal week look like when you are living in community on mission as a worshipful image bearer?

Take the time to address these issues as you craft a vivid picture of what it looks like, by the grace of God to live out your calling to follow Jesus.

As a shepherd, it is your role to keep these kinds of questions and priorities in the windshield view of your disciples. Do not let them settle for something merely manageable. Instead, graciously call them to action that requires their lives to express grace. Their identity is not in what they do, but they reflect their functional identity by what they are doing. Call them to their gospel identity. As they form their action plans, call them to specifics—names, dates, particular actions. If we drift off mission with specific neglects, preoccupations, and misplaced priorities, we will live unfocused lives with generic life plans. Help disciples craft the specifics of the coming week and month; help them evaluate their past month based on how Jesus was followed. Was he imaged and worshiped well? Were others loved in community and on mission? This is leading as a shepherd in the life of a disciple.

When done well, shepherding will call people upward in their pursuit of Jesus. Disciples will seek God for the direction to set faith goals for their lives, as well as for divine empowerment to follow Jesus. Grace without action can degenerate into enablement or encouraging disciples merely to "do their best" or to "keep trying." Shepherding is all about exposing grace as God's delivery system for life change. "Or do you presume on the riches of his kindness and forbearance and patience, not knowing that God's kindness is meant to lead you to repentance?" (Rom. 2:4).

Quadrant 4: Truth + Deed = Protecting

As a disciple there are certain elements you should establish in your game plan. The first is repentance. No disciple shoots 100 percent. Learning the skill and discipline of rebounding is a criti-

The unexamined life is not worth living. —Socrates

cal component to learning to "score" as a disciple. Repentance is the disciple's rebound.

John writes, "If we confess our sins, he is faithful and just to forgive us our sins and to cleanse us from all unrighteousness" (1 John 1:9). This verse tells us that God's grace is greater than a 1:1 correspondence between confession and forgiveness. He invites a heart of confession, and his grace forgives far more than we confess. His grace forgives all our unrighteousness. Confession is embracing God's truth regarding our actions and our hearts. The truth is that we sin (1 John 1:10). We default to ourselves and our idols over God at a staggering rate. Confession is repenting of declaring God as not good or enough to fill our hearts. When we name God as God—as more than sufficient—he cleanses us of all the ways we have disrespected him without our even knowing it.

A second element or strategy to your game plan is how to deal with temptation. Christians must learn to escape temptation:

> No temptation has overtaken you that is not common to man. God is faithful, and he will not let you be tempted beyond your ability, but with the temptation he will also provide the way of escape, that you may be able to endure it. (1 Cor. 10:13)
>
> So flee youthful passions and pursue righteousness, faith, love, and peace, along with those who call on the Lord from a pure heart. (2 Tim. 2:22)

The Scriptures are clear that when a disciple recognizes temptation, the strategy is to find the nearest exit. As you assess your sticking points, as well as your personality, you will become aware of some unique temptations, and maybe strongholds will surface. Here are a few common ones: anger, fear, depression, and lust. There may be some specific behaviors that you will have to guard yourself from: alcohol and substance abuse, gambling, lying, spending, escapism through video games, TV and movies, romance novels, working to escape coming home—the list goes on. As you identify your personal temptations, you will need to devise a defense strategy that allows you to flee from temptation.

My wife Sue and I lived for over fifty years without knowing each other. I was married to Jeanne for more than thirty years, and Sue was a single mom for over twenty years. As a result, our backgrounds collide as we approach problem solving. We have had to develop a way of avoiding the temptation to fight through our decisions. We realized that we process things differently; our pace in making decisions is different, and our comfort with others' knowing the decisions we face is different. In short, we were letting the need to make a decision be more important than how we made decisions. So we developed a trust behavior: when we feel the temperature rising, or the situation is militating against our making a decision together, we say, "Pass," and postpone the discussion and decision. Surely this can be abused as an avoidance tactic, and that is why I said it is a trust behavior between us. It has served us well in pledging to one another that oneness between us is more important than winning, fighting, or deciding. This simple strategy is a discipleship defense for guarding community between the two of us.

Not only are there pitfalls based on you and your life, but also there is a spiritual battle, and we find ourselves in the midst of it. Paul spends significant time in Ephesians 6 talking about the armor of God, which includes truth, righteousness, faith, salvation, the gospel of peace, and the Word of God. While these components in and of themselves speak to the pursuit of Jesus, Paul links them to a cosmic battle against Satan. He suggests that this armor of God is given to disciples so that we may stand against the schemes of the Devil.

> Put on the whole armor of God, that you may be able to stand against the schemes of the devil. (Eph. 6:11)

Many have taken these verses to suggest that believers are to engage in an offensive spiritual battle against the Devil. But

Paul here specifically identifies the armor as a defense against his strategies. In Ephesians 4 Paul suggests that the reason for keeping short accounts and not leaving unresolved anger until the next day is that it gives the Devil an opportunity (vv. 26–27). Therefore, as disciples we are responsible to clothe ourselves in the character of Christ, empowered by the Holy Spirit, since there is an enemy of our soul who seeks to derail us as Christ followers (1 Pet. 5:8–9).

James too mentions resisting the Devil:

> Submit yourselves therefore to God. Resist the devil, and he will flee from you. Draw near to God, and he will draw near to you. (James 4:7–8)

James couples our resistance with a humble proximity to God, which is akin to putting on the armor of God, rather than self-help and behavior modification. As a disciple it is important to know that a Spirit-filled life is our best defense against attempting to live a life powered on the lesser resource of the flesh (Gal. 5:16–25).

As disciples, we must develop discernment to realize when we are being influenced by our flesh and to flee, and a discernment to realize when we are being influenced by the Enemy and resist so that he will flee. Having someone else speak into what this looks like is exactly what it means to enlist the protective role of a shepherd-coach.

Another warning light to monitor is self-sufficiency. Perhaps the best way to monitor our dependence upon God is our prayer life. Prayer is much more than requests; it is thanksgiving and gratitude:

> Rejoice always, pray without ceasing, give thanks in all circumstances; for this is the will of God in Christ Jesus for you. Do not quench the Spirit. (1 Thess. 5:16–19)

To live a prayerful life is to live a life of following Jesus.

All these are the disciple's skills of self-defense. A protective shepherd-coach does well to help disciples identify the threats to their walk with God. I have spent too many hours with people asking "safe" questions of each other, thinking they are protecting their souls, when in reality they are asking questions at the most guarded entry points of the soul, leaving vulnerable places unsecured. For example, men with whom I am in community pose questions about sexuality and finances. It's not that any of us are above or beyond being tempted to derailment and spiritual destruction in these areas; it's just that these concerns are often the ones we spend time building security systems around to prevent a breach, while we continue to struggle daily with pride, greed, and gossip.

Jerry Bridges has authored a book entitled *Respectable Sins: Confronting the Sins We Tolerate.*[2] The upshot of the book is that we tolerate sins like pride, selfishness, and ingratitude, but we have a strong moral objection to sins like adultery, homosexuality, or drunkenness. The question must be asked: Is our toleration based on our involvement in sin, whereas our revulsion is based on our perception that we are not likely to commit certain reprehensible sins? Do we think that perhaps we can manage and modify our way into respectability, recalibrating discipleship to look like religious morality rather than like the life of Jesus?

A good shepherd will help the disciple identify what is toxic to his soul. Several times, the image of shepherd in the Scriptures speaks of sheep being led to green pastures. I can't imagine a shepherd being called "good" who had led his sheep to a field of poisonous berries and allowed his sheep to feed to their own peril. Disciples must develop a life plan that includes avoiding the deadly intake of religious behavior.

This step beyond sin avoidance brings us to the issue of idols. A shepherd is willing to help the disciple face "the sin behind the sin." While someone may struggle with anger, what makes that person angry may be pride. Someone else may struggle with lust, but what is going on in the heart is a selfish lack of gratitude for the spouse God has provided. A shepherd protects a disciple from stopping at sin avoidance and behavior adjusting by drilling down to the heart as the only means of helping the disciple experience freedom from sin's enslaving domain.

As a disciple you must own your calling to follow Jesus. Putting together a life plan imaging God as a worshiper in community on mission is your charge. Finding a disciple who can help you as a shepherd-coach is part of what it means to walk as Jesus did. Set aside some time in the next couple of weeks to envision what it would look like to live your life fulfilling God's call in your life. Ask God for direction and discernment about who you might ask to share this daring vision with, and ask him or her to join you as shepherd-coach. Don't let skepticism or fear rob you of the abundant life Jesus envisions for his followers.

> I am the door. If anyone enters by me, he will be saved and will go in and out and find pasture. The thief comes only to steal and kill and destroy. I came that they may have life and have it abundantly. I am the good shepherd. The good shepherd lays down his life for the sheep. (John 10:9–11)

CHAPTER 11 ASSIGNMENT

Encounter

1) Do a character study of Obed-edom. He was an Old Testament priest whose life was changed by his encounter with the ark (2 Samuel 6; 1 Chronicles 13).

2) As you consider Obed-edom's life, how much of a priority was it for him to serve God?

3) What kind of legacy did Obed-edom leave to his family?

Explore

Paul told Timothy, "You then, my child, be strengthened by the grace that is in Christ Jesus, and what you have heard from me in the presence of many witnesses entrust to faithful men who will be able to teach others also" (2 Tim. 2:1–2). Below you will find exercises designed to help you assess what you have heard and make it something you can entrust to faithful people who will in turn teach others.

1) In chapter 11 you were exposed to the idea of "sticking points." Take some time to review this concept, then take a personal inventory of the sticking points that are keeping you from moving forward as a disciple.

2) In chapter 11 it was suggested that you make a plan to expose yourself to the person and teachings of Jesus. You might consider reading through the Bible in a year or finding a book or study that walks through the life of Jesus. You might decide to study his parables or read about his miracles. Whatever you decide to implement, develop rhythm on a daily or weekly cycle, such as daily prayer and Bible reading. You might decide to pray for friends on Mondays, for your community group on Tuesdays, for your pastor on Wednesdays, for those with whom you work or go to school on Thursdays, and for opportunities to share Jesus on Fridays. On Saturdays you might pray that your heart will be prepared to worship God on Sunday and that God will use you in the lives of others at church.

3) As you prepare yourself to be used by God to disciple someone, take a half day to reflect on what you have had to learn in order to follow Jesus. You are the curriculum God is going to use.

4) Make a compelling word picture of what it means to follow Jesus. Include areas of your life such as finances, gifts, talents, and strengths, and your rhythms of worship, community, and mission.

5) You were challenged in chapter 11 to think of ways to escape temptations. What temptations do you consistently face? What defenses do you currently have in place? Whom do you need to recruit as partners in your escape strategies?

12

MULTIPLICATION

Reading a last chapter—I wonder how many people make it here? I have gone through more than my fair share of half-read books, and have bought many used books that were not highlighted past the first couple of chapters. To ignore this chapter, however, would be a tragedy in your pursuit of disciple making, for Jesus expected that his disciples would make disciples.[1] The process is not mere division of labor, such as when Jethro advised his son-in-law, Moses, to deploy able, God-fearing men to join him in the venture of administering justice to the people of Israel (Ex. 18:21–22). The concept of "division of labor" is quite different from the challenge Paul issued to Timothy: "You then, my child, be strengthened by the grace that is in Christ Jesus, and what you have heard from me in the presence of many witnesses entrust to faithful men who will be able to teach others also" (2 Tim. 2:1–2). Division of labor has to do with resource management; disciple making has to do with expanding God's kingdom and the power of the gospel: "For I am not ashamed of the gospel, for it is the power of God for salvation to everyone who believes, to the Jew first and also to the Greek. For in it the righteousness of God is revealed from faith for faith," (Rom. 1:16–17).

In commissioning disciples to make disciples, Jesus invited people to their role in his story. As we have already seen in Jesus's prayer in John 17, he envisioned his disciples with a contagious faith: "As you sent me into the world, so I have sent them into the world . . . that they may all be one, just as you, Father, are in me, and I in you, that they also may be in us, so that the world may believe that you have sent me" (John 17:18, 21). Jesus sent his disciples on mission as he was sent on mission, believing that displaying the gospel would have a redemptive impact in the world.

In Matthew 28, where we find the Great Commission, Jesus included the specific instruction to teach disciples to observe what he had commanded (v. 20), but he meant much more than merely teaching his commands. The litmus test of disciple making is observing Jesus's commands, not simply being aware of Jesus's commands. It requires imparting skills from one life to another. Let's look at a few examples.

Prayer

First, Jesus commanded us to pray (Matt. 6:5–13). I am pretty sure most Christians know this, but I am also pretty sure most Christians stumble through their prayers, wondering if they are praying like Jesus or have prayed in Jesus's name, or have done little more than launch a wish to God like a message in a bottle being sent out to sea. Teaching people to observe Jesus's command to pray includes praying for and over people so that they might truly experience someone lifting their concerns and needs to God. As people experience this, they will become more at ease in praying for and over others. They receive an imprinted pattern for what they are supposed to do.

Several years ago I was faced with the need to decide whether to lead my family of six away from a paid ministry position, across the country with no employer, on a church planting venture. I was speaking at a youth conference north of Toronto and had several friends, serious intercessors, who lived nearby. My wife and I agreed that it would be okay to take an extra day after the conference and ask these friends to gather and pray over me and the decision I was facing.

The prayer time was intense and in many ways unique to the

people and setting, but during that time, one man took some oil, put it on his finger, made the symbol of a cross on my forehead, and prayed that the peace of God would transcend my understanding. A little over a year later, I was in Seattle gathering a core to plant a church. To provide some income streams to our family, I had taken on a consulting role with a church. During my time with that church, a woman suffering from cancer for many years was going in for a surgery and had asked the elders to come and pray over her. The elders asked if I would join them. I asked if anyone was bringing oil, and so they did.

When we arrived at the woman's house, I asked her if it would be all right if we anointed her with oil. She laughed and said, "Not again!" It seems the last time these elders had come, they had doused her with an entire bottle of cooking oil as they sought to apply James 5:14. I assured her that we would use less oil this time. I put some oil on my index finger, set her hands palms up on her knees, made the sign of the cross on her forehead, and tapped oil on her palms as we prayed that the peace of God would transcend her understanding and that she would receive God's healing. After our prayer time we piled in the van and drove back toward the church with the elders laughing about their previous "oiling" and how simple yet significant our prayer time had been. These elders had already understood their assignment, but no one had ever shown them a way to observe their charge from James.

Praying also includes praising God for who he is and what he has done. I am surprised how many people say to me, "If God is in control, then why do I need to pray?" If I detect anger underlying that question, I try to get to the root of their anger and mistrust. If they are asking sincerely, I might say, "Does your prayer life consist only of requests?" If God is in control, then there are millions of things to thank him for: light, color, water, sound, birds, and life.

I like to take a buzzer or a bell to prayer meetings and sound this device whenever one of us makes a request. I challenge the group to see how long we can talk to God without asking him for something. It is a very telling exercise as we weigh our words and try to talk to God for even five minutes without asking God to do something for us. Yet we are told to thank God and give him praise. Again, most Christians know this, but we have to be equipped to practice it.

In my journal I use a pen with green ink to record praises and things for which I am grateful. I even take time at least once a week to read over the requests I have recorded, and write next to the requests any ways I have observed God acting. On the days I feel down, going on a hunt for green in my journal is a productive way to pursue the building up of my faith. It is our disciple-making responsibility to go beyond disciplining ourselves to sharing our best practices with other disciples.

Shaped by the Word

Second, Jesus commands us to be shaped by the Word of God: "So Jesus said to the Jews who had believed in him, 'If you abide in my word, you are truly my disciples, and you will know the truth, and the truth will set you free'" (John 8:31–32). Here are a few simple categories to keep in mind as you are reading the Bible: (1) sins to confess; (2) promises to claim; (3) examples to follow or avoid; (4) commands to obey; (5) statements of significance. These five points are easy to remember as SPECS. There are many helpful books on ways to study the Bible, from a hermeneutical approach to actual topical and book studies. There is value to undertaking an inductive method of Bible study. This includes making observations about the text, seeking to see what it actually says and how it would have been understood by the original audience. This is one of the hardest ways to begin Bible study. I am so quick to seek what it means to me that I shortchange myself and often miss some of the richness of the Bible by failing to slow down and see what the passage actually says.

Once I have spent some time reading the passage, I set about to determine who is involved in the passage or where and when the event took place.

Take, for example, the psalm attributed to King David with the verse, "The LORD is in his holy temple" (Ps. 11:4). It is helpful to know that David longed to build God a temple and was denied the privilege, suggesting that "his holy temple" is something other than the temple Solomon his son built in Jerusalem after David's death.

These observations set me in the specifics of the historical lives and times in which the Scriptures were written. From there, I want to discern general principles that speak across historical and cultural specifics. In other words, how does the passage relate to the story of God? After I have wrestled with that, I try to bring the truths back to the specifics of my world and context. I move from the timeless truths of God's story to timely application of those truths to me in God's story. This is where SPECS focuses. A disciple is someone who is constantly working at having a better understanding of the Scriptures: "Do your best to present yourself to God as one approved, a worker who has no need to be ashamed, rightly handling the word of truth" (2 Tim. 2:15).

Forgiveness

Third, Jesus commands us to forgive. The passages are many where Jesus pronounces forgiveness to people, and that was one of the primary offenses the religious people of his day had against him (see, e.g., Luke 5:17–26). Peter asked Jesus to tell him how many times he had to forgive in order to be a righteous man. Peter thought seven was a righteous number, but Jesus went beyond even seventy times and told Peter the right number is seventy times seven (Matt. 18:21–22). This was not so that Peter would forgive someone 490 times, but so that Peter could understand that forgiveness is itself a grace that God bestows on his people to be disclosed and displayed to others by his disciples joining Jesus on mission. Offering forgiveness might open up an occasion for the gospel as well and, in fact, it is one of the most profound ways of incarnating our declaration of the gospel.

The apostle Paul is an incredible model of one who multiplied disciples. The list of those whom he led to discipleship is staggering. Add to it the realization that they were all first-generation Christians, and it is nothing less than supernatural. None of these early disciples had grown up in a family, church, or culture in which the gospel had been proclaimed. The church and the message of reconciliation through the person and work of Jesus were being rolled out for the first time through the message of Paul, the other apostles, and pockets of believers living out the gospel in frontier mission posts called "church."

Both through their lives and teachings, Jesus and Paul demonstrated the priority of going to people who do not know of Jesus and his kingdom. This going must be both local and global. Locally, each of us is to join God in speaking to those with whom we share life—at work, at home, and in our neighborhoods— and in community service. Paul articulates his urgency for presenting the gospel as he morphed his lifestyle to build bridges from his life to others:

> For though I am free from all, I have made myself a servant to all, that I might win more of them. To the Jews I became as a Jew, in order to win Jews. To those under the law I became as one under the law (though not being myself under the law) that I might win those under the law. To those outside the law I became as one outside the law (not being outside the law of God but under the law of Christ) that I might win those outside the law. To the weak I became weak, that I might win the weak. I have become all things to all people, that by all means I might save some. I do it all for the sake of the gospel, that I may share with them in its blessings. (1 Cor. 9:19–23)

What I find intriguing are the differing motives for the same behavior. I know many Christians who take on a kind of chameleon-like behavior, as did Paul—under the law, outside the law, weak, all things to all people—but they lack the self-surrender that Paul demonstrated: "that by all means I might save some." Their behavior is often the very opposite of that. It is to fit in and avoid being rejected, laughed at, or marginalized because they are Christians. When people seek to fit in, they might as well say, "That by all means I might save myself." Paul and Jesus were both willing to die to themselves to see others experience reconciliation to God and the transforming work of the Holy Spirit.

Jesus expresses the need for reconciliation by telling sequential stories in Luke 15 of a lost sheep, a lost coin, and a lost son. Each story speaks of a sacrificial search and a celebration when what is lost is found. Jesus obviously goes far beyond teaching in calling for reconciliation as life's priority. He experienced death that we might experience life. Unfortunately, many people long to see others accept Jesus but give little thought to people following Jesus. Jesus invites people to follow him, not to accept him:

> While walking by the Sea of Galilee, he saw two brothers, Simon (who is called Peter) and Andrew his brother, casting a net into the sea, for they were fishermen. And he said to them, "Follow me, and I will make you fishers of men." Immediately they left their nets and followed him. (Matt. 4:18–20)
>
> As Jesus passed on from there, he saw a man called Matthew sitting at the tax booth, and he said to him, "Follow me." And he rose and followed him. (Matt. 9:9)
>
> Then Jesus told his disciples, "If anyone would come after me, let him deny himself and take up his cross and follow me." (Matt. 16:24)
>
> Again Jesus spoke to them, saying, "I am the light of the world. Whoever follows me will not walk in darkness, but will have the light of life." (John 8:12)

The concept of *following* evokes rich imagery—journey, process, adventure, and dependence. *Accepting* sounds like Jesus is put on our scales, and we decide his fate, like he is campaigning for our vote as he runs for Messiah. To accept Jesus does not call one to live as a disciple; it merely calls one to make a decision. Following calls for a series of decisions being made by the minute, keeping Jesus the focal point, refusing to look to the right or the left, increasing in likeness to his character and in closeness to his person.

To go into the world and call others to make decisions is to take on the challenge of selling a product called "Christianity." To go into the world and make disciples is to take on the challenge of partnering with God as agents of grace, introducing people to a lifelong journey of following the life, truth, and way to reconciliation with God. So what does it take to be a disciple maker?

A Servant's Heart

Being a disciple is all about you and Jesus. Being a disciple maker is about Jesus and someone else. In the West we know little of servanthood; we know more about the distortions of slavery. In Jesus's day, servants were those who actually received social identity from their masters. Here are a couple of examples of what I mean. In an agricultural setting, wealth and status were measured in land ownership, not in function. So a wealthy land owner might send a servant to medical school so that there was a doctor on the estate. In an urban setting, a wealthy man might have had his servant well educated and then assigned to educate the young men of the household. In our world and thinking, a slave is someone who is mistreated, uneducated, and poorly cared for. A slave would have little reason to willfully stay enslaved to a harsh slave owner, but a servant who is well treated and commissioned to care for family, nurture minds, and invest in a heritage may very well decide this is a worthy life's calling.

It requires such a heart to be a disciple maker. What is the payoff for those who worship God, get their identity in Jesus, and live life in community, using their resources to join God on mission? For servants, it is tied to their love and devotion to their master. For disciple makers, while we serve those we disciple, joy and strength-giving endurance come from their love and devotion to Jesus. We serve Jesus when we equip others to follow him with surrendered lives rather than get others to cast a vote of acceptance for him as Savior of the world.

disciple makers - plan
- learn
. . Examples/encourages
- osmosis but natural
- catch

A Visionary Mindset

A disciple maker must be someone who can see what is not there. This doesn't mean projecting what will never be and living an envisioned fantasy. It means that God has framed out what we can expect life to look like when we follow Jesus, and a disciple maker works from that template, imparting Christlikeness as a vision worth living for.

Several years ago, I bought a house that was nearly one hundred years old and in terrible condition. The neighborhood was so bad that the state was giving low-interest loans to people who would move into it. As my wife, three little children, and mother surveyed the house, it was interesting to see the different reactions. My mother saw a house like one she had lived in many years prior. My wife saw a kitchen without dishwasher, garbage disposal, or appliances. My children saw winding staircases and hiding places. I saw lath and plaster, old wiring, peeling paint, and one bathroom for the six of us. So why did we buy the house? My wife saw a big kitchen and a dining room that could entertain, my mom saw a bedroom on the main floor without stairs, I saw where another bathroom could go in and how my high school youth group would love demolishing walls, and my kids saw adventurous stairs and hiding places. The point is that we bought the house based on a vision, not on its condition. A disciple will seldom engage someone without being able to envision where it will lead.

Listen to Jesus as he cast a vision for his disciples. When

Jesus met Nathanael, their interaction convinced Nathanael that Jesus is the son of God. Jesus raised Nathanael's sights and said to him, "Because I said to you, 'I saw you under the fig tree,' do you believe? You will see greater things than these" (John 1:50). To Peter he changed his name (John 1:42); to four fishermen he raised the bar from fish to men as the catch of the day (Matt. 4:18–22; Mark 1:16–20).

A Loving Concern

Paul's description of love is most often read at weddings, and it is not put in the context of being a litmus test for the legitimacy of one's motive for ministry. Paul paints a picture of over-the-top ministry expressions and then explains that each is worthless if it isn't motivated by love:

> If I speak in the tongues of men and of angels, but have not love, I am a noisy gong or a clanging cymbal. And if I have prophetic powers, and understand all mysteries and all knowledge, and if I have all faith, so as to remove mountains, but have not love, I am nothing. If I give away all I have, and if I deliver up my body to be burned, but have not love, I gain nothing. Love is patient and kind; love does not envy or boast; it is not arrogant or rude. It does not insist on its own way; it is not irritable or resentful; it does not rejoice at wrongdoing, but rejoices with the truth. Love bears all things, believes all things, hopes all things, endures all things. Love never ends. (1 Cor. 13:1–8)

Paul then goes on to give a compelling picture of what love is like. It is noteworthy that this description is in the middle of his description of spiritual gifts. It is as though Paul is pointing out that the Corinthian believers have been finding their identity in the gifts they'd been given. The Corinthians are examples to us all of how easy it is to gain identity from gifting rather than from the one we serve with our gifts. Paul does a masterful job of calling the Corinthians to a higher ground by describing the very love Jesus modeled.

What if we front-loaded a call to disciple making with a litany of accomplishments? If I could call thousands to live by Jesus's priorities, if there were hundreds of churches planted, if there were shelters and day care programs established, but there is no love, what score do you think Paul would give it? Loving God and loving others is the bumper-sticker version of Jesus's mission statement. If we disciple others without loving God or loving them, the likelihood is they will be our disciples rather than Jesus's disciples. It will be impossible to communicate to them a compelling reason to follow Jesus whatever the cost if he is esteemed but not loved. It will be easy for disciples to pass on getting together in community if they think they are part of a project rather than people who are loved. This heart of love is Paul's apostolic DNA.[2]

To the Corinthians, Paul writes that he was controlled or compelled by the love of Christ; he had no option but to do what the love of Jesus would demand of him. To Timothy, his disciple, he writes that the aim of our charge or the goal of our disciple-making efforts is love. As a disciple-making disciple, you must have a heart condition, and the condition of your heart must be that of a loving visionary servant.

Finally, I would like to suggest that the difference between discipleship and indoctrination is spiritual direction. To disciple people is not to make them like everybody else; it is to shape them into the image of Jesus. "Every Christian is a disciple of Jesus because in the kingdom of God it is only Jesus who has disciples."[3] So even though we agree on identity aspects of imaging God, worshiping God, living in community as the people of God, and joining God on mission, this is really in the letters of our alphabet, but following Jesus as his disciple in our circumstances and relationships becomes our personal signature that everyone must use. A disciple maker, then, is one who can use these identity components in helping a disciple close the gap to observing Jesus's commands.

Being a disciple maker, then, means prayerful dependence upon the Holy Spirit for his guidance in discernment. It is much more than simply putting a calendar and goals together; it involves listening for the disciple's areas of needed transformation. Let's say you are going to disciple two men in your community group. Both men are in their mid-twenties, and both men have similar educational backgrounds and jobs. One man is single, and the other has been married for eight months. Community looks different in the lives of these two men. For the single man, community might include letting people speak with authority into his life. For a newly married man, community might be about learning to see the world from "us" and "we" instead of "me" and "I." So, as disciple maker, you might ask your single disciple to identify a way he will join in some kind of activity with his community that he may not have chosen on his own. For your newly married disciple, you might ask him to involve his wife in a decision. The purpose of these assignments is to get both men to grow in their understanding of imaging Jesus as someone who did not act autonomously: "So Jesus said to them, 'Truly, truly, I say to you, the Son can do nothing of his own accord, but only what he sees the Father doing. For whatever the Father does, that the Son does likewise'" (John 5:19).

Paul tells us that though Jesus is God, he took on the nature of both man and servant. We are told several places in the record of Jesus's praying in the garden before his crucifixion that pleasing the Father and surrendering to his will was what Jesus was all about. What would it look like to make disciples shaped with this same mentality? We would see men and women who could help each other walk away from enslaving relationships and habits; men and women who were willing to give up their own time to serve others. It will not happen by making everyone look the same but rather by having everyone love and serve with the same vision of greater things being done through them.

While calling disciples to similarly imaging God through

worship, some will express themselves through creatively using their talents, and others will see their need to give their resources sacrificially. Both want God to be seen as creator and provider. Both want to be on God's mission to bring about his kingdom through the gospel message and the gospel community of his people. It's his story, and we're in it.

> And the whole story is predicated on the reality of this God and the mission of this God. He is the originator of the story, the teller of the story, the prime actor in the story, the planner and guide of the story's plot, the meaning of the story and its ultimate completion. He is its beginning, end and center. It is the story of the mission of God, of this God and no other.[4]

It is my sincere hope that in your journey to live and love like Jesus, you will leave in your wake many disciples living out their gospel identity. I pray you will find the grace to embrace your role in God's story, imaging Jesus as the true hero he is, worshiping the Trinity as the worthy God they are, loving others in the community called "Christ's body," and joining God in telling his story throughout his planet and your generation. Who would have thought that life's most profound meaning could be had by simply responding to his invitation, "Follow me"?

were you effectively discipled by an individual?

"do it my way" - really?

CHAPTER 12 ASSIGNMENT

Read the account of Jesus calling his first disciples (John 1:35–51). Take time to journal and reflect on the vision of these thirty gospel beneficiaries of Paul's ministry in Romans 16. Make a list of thirty people you hope will hear and receive the message of the gospel.

Explore

1) Read Luke 9–10. What instructions, authority, and expectations were given to those Jesus sent out? What is needed for you to be sent as a disciple maker, to send out other disciples?

2) According to Acts 6, do you think the first deacons were capable of making disciples? How do you think they developed to their level of maturity? Does this help you develop a disciple-making strategy?

3) As you read John 1, what do you learn about John the Baptist as a disciple maker?

4) Read Romans 16. How many people does Paul list as partnering with him in the cause of the gospel? What does this say about making disciples through community?

5) Take the time to do a character study of Barnabas in the book of Acts. How did God use him to advance the kingdom? When Barnabas and Paul parted ways (Acts 15), what did Barnabas do? What do you think Barnabas saw as his life's calling?

Digging Deeper

As you look at the character studies in the chart below, think of other experiences in each of these men's lives that you would put in the chart.

	David	Elijah	Daniel	Jesus	Peter	Paul
Image	Confronts Goliath (1 Sam. 17:36–37, 45–47)	Man of God (1 Kings 17)	Resolved to keep himself set apart for God (Dan. 1:3–17)	Transfiguration (Matt. 17:1–7)	Where would we go? (John 6:68)	Damascus road (Acts 9)
Worship	Dances before the Lord (2 Sam. 6:16–21)	Confronts King Ahab about idolatry (2 Kings 1)	Continued prayer life even when illegal (Dan. 6:1–10)	Prayer in the garden (Matt. 26:36–46)	Walking on water (Matt. 14:22–33)	Singing in jail (Acts 16:25–34)
Community	Bonds with his mighty men (2 Sam. 23:15–17)	Relationship with his disciple Elisha (2 Kings 2:1–14)	Shares life with companions (Dan. 2:17–18)	Upper room (John 14–16)	Foot washing (John 13:1–20)	Limit freedom for a weaker brother (1 Corinthians 8)
Mission	Psalm 24 spans generations and sees the Lord as the king of earth.	Calls nation to repent as God defeats its idol Baal (1 Kings 18)	Points the king to God as the source of wisdom (Dan. 2:26–28)	Matthew's dinner (Matt. 9:9–13)	Takes the gospel to Gentiles (Acts 10)	Commissioned with Barnabas and sent out (Acts 13:1–4)

NOTES

Chapter 1: The Story of God

1. Graeme Goldsworthy, *According to Plan: The Unfolding Revelations of God in the Bible* (Downers Grove, IL: InterVarsity, 1991), 32.

2. John Frame, *The Doctrine of God* (Phillipsburg, NJ: P&R, 2002), 154–59.

3. Anthony Hoekema, *Created in God's Image* (Grand Rapids, MI: Eerdmans, 1986), 6.

4. John Calvin, *Institutes of the Christian Religion*, trans. Henry Beveridge (Peabody, MA: Hendrickson, 2008), 1.5.1.

5. Wayne Grudem defines the sufficiency of Scripture this way: "[It] means that Scripture contained all the words of God he intended his people to have at each stage of redemptive history, and that it now contains all the words of God we need for salvation, for trusting him perfectly, and for obeying him perfectly." Taken from Grudem's *Systematic Theology: An Introduction to Biblical Doctrine* (Grand Rapids, MI: Zondervan, 1994), 127.

6. "God eternally exists as three persons, Father, Son, and Holy Spirit, and each person is fully God, and there is one God." Taken from Grudem's *Systematic Theology*, 226.

7. "Therefore a man shall leave his father and his mother and hold fast to his wife, and they shall become one flesh" (Gen. 2:24).

8. Bruce A. Ware, *Father, Son, and Holy Spirit: Relationships, Roles, and Relevance* (Wheaton, IL: Crossway, 2005), 133.

9. Bruce A. Ware states, "To understand God as triune is also to see more clearly what creaturely life is meant to be." For more in-depth study, read chap. 6 in his *Father, Son, and Holy Spirit*, 131–58.

10. Grudem, *Systematic Theology: An Introduction to Biblical Doctrine*, 413.

11. For a full treatment of the garden of Eden as it relates to the cosmic battle and the creation/fall narrative, see chap. 3 in Stephen G. Dempster's *Dominion and Dynasty: A Theology of the Hebrew Bible*, New Studies in Biblical Theology 15, ed. D. A. Carson (Downers Grove, IL: InterVarsity, 2003).

12. See John Piper, "I Will Magnify God with Thanksgiving," http://www.desiringgod.org/resource.library/sermons/i-will-magnify-god-with-thanksgiving.

13. Timothy Keller, *Counterfeit Gods: The Empty Promises of Money, Sex, and Power, and the Only Hope that Matters* (New York: Dutton, 2009), *xvii*.

14. "In 1990 a star named the Pistol Star was known to lie at the center of the Pistol Nebula. In 1995 it was suggested that the Pistol Star was so massive it was throwing off the mass that actually created the Pistol Nebula. Now, observations from the Hubble Space Telescope released today confirm the spectral relation between the star and the nebula. Dramatic implications include that the star emits 10 million times more light than our Sun, and is about 100 times more massive. Astronomers are currently unsure how a star this massive could have formed and how it will act in the future." Taken from http://antwrp.gsfc.nasa.gov/apod/ap971008.html.

15. Graeme Goldsworthy, *According to Plan*, 137.

16. Dietrich Bonhoeffer, *Life Together* (San Francisco: HarperSanFrancisco, 1954), 23.

17. Tim Chester and Steve Timmis, *Total Church: A Radical Reshaping around Gospel and Community* (Wheaton, IL: Crossway, 2009), 63.

18. Taken from Andreas J. Köstenberger and Scott R. Swain, *Father, Son and Spirit: The Trinity and John's Gospel*. Copyright © Andreas J. Köstenberger and Scott R. Swain, 2008. Used by permission of InterVarsity Press PO Box 1400 Downers Grove, IL 60515. http://www.ivpress.com.

Chapter 2: The Hero of the Story

1. For detecting and discerning common fallacies in Bible study, see D. A. Carson, *Exegetical Fallacies*, 2nd ed. (Grand Rapids, MI: Baker, 2005). Concerning the present topic, see pp. 125–36, in particular. For instance, proof-texting often occurs when "reading one's personal theology into the text" (p. 128).

2. Mark Driscoll, *On the Old Testament*, A Book You'll Actually Read (Wheaton, IL: Crossway, 2008), 34–40.

3. Andreas J. Köstenberger and Scott R. Swain, *Father, Son and Spirit: The Trinity and John's Gospel*, New Studies in Biblical Theology 24, ed. D. A. Carson (Downers Grove, IL: InterVarsity Press, 2008), 113.

4. John Piper, *The Pleasures of God: Meditations on God's Delight in Being God* (Sisters, OR: Multnomah, 2000), 138.

5. Anthony Hoekema, *Created in God's Image* (Grand Rapids, MI: Eerdmans, 1986), 22.

6. For a full explanation, see Bruce A. Ware, *God's Greater Glory: The Exalted God of Scripture and the Christian Faith* (Wheaton, IL: Crossway, 2004), 85–95.

Chapter 3: Image

1. Anthony Hoekema, *Created in God's Image* (Grand Rapids, MI: Eerdmans, 1986), 75.

2. Ibid., 32.

3. Ibid., 26.

4. As we have already mentioned, in Job 1 Satan comes before God, and God tells him to look at Job as someone who pleases him. Also, Peter tells us that angels long to look in to the saving story God is working out in his people (1 Pet. 1:12).

5. "Then Job arose and tore his robe and shaved his head and fell on the ground and worshiped. And he said, 'Naked I came from my mother's womb, and naked shall I return. The LORD gave, and the LORD has taken away; blessed be the name of the LORD'" (Job 1:20–21).

6. Paul E. Miller, *A Praying Life: Connecting with God in a Distracting World* (Colorado Springs, CO: NavPress, 2009), 90.

7. Lewis Sperry Chafer, *Chafer Systematic Theology: Soteriology*, vol. 3 (Dallas: Dallas Seminary Press, 1983), 234–65.

Chapter 4: Identity Distortions

1. Anthony Hoekema, *Created in God's Image* (Grand Rapids, MI: Eerdmans, 1986), 85.

2. Timothy Keller, *The Prodigal God: Recovering the Heart of the Christian Faith* (New York: Dutton, 2008), 70–71.

3. In his *Institutes*, Calvin lays out the implications of hypocrisy: "In short, while their confidence ought to have been fixed upon him, they put him aside, and rest in themselves or the creatures. At length they bewilder themselves in such a maze of error, that the darkness of ignorance obscures, and ultimately extinguishes, those sparks which were designed to show them the glory of God" (John Calvin, *Institutes of the Christian Religion*, trans. Henry Beveridge [Peabody, MA: Hendrickson Publishers, 2008], 1.4.4).

4. Bruce A. Ware points out that the power of contrary choice or "libertarian freedom is often referred to as a 'freedom of indifference,'" and in it, "we are strictly indifferent to whether we choose A or not-A, since the reason or reasons we have for one are identical to the reason or reasons we have for the other" (*God's Greater Glory: The Exalted God of Scripture and the Christian Faith* [Wheaton, IL: Crossway, 2004], 86).

5. C. S. Lewis, *The Problem of Pain* (New York: Macmillan, 1962), 93.

Chapter 5: Worship

1. Harold M. Best, *Unceasing Worship: Biblical Perspectives on Worship and the Arts* (Downers Grove, IL: InterVarsity, 2003), 47.

2. Bob Kauflin, *Worship Matters: Leading Others to Encounter the Greatness of God* (Wheaton, IL: Crossway, 2008), 70.

3. David Peterson, *Engaging with God: a Biblical Theology of Worship* (Downers Grove, IL: InterVarsity, 1992), 99.

4. John Piper, *Desiring God: Meditations of a Christian Hedonist* (Sisters, OR: Multnomah, 2003), 27.

5. Andreas J. Köstenberger and Scott R. Swain, *Father, Son and Spirit: The Trinity and John's Gospel*, New Studies in Biblical Theology 24, ed. D. A. Carson (Downers Grove, IL: InterVarsity, 2008), 178; italics original.

6. Peterson, *Engaging with God*, 32.

7. See, e.g., http//www.doxawatches.com.

8. Peterson, *Engaging with God*, 67.

Chapter 6: Worship Distortions

1. "And the haughtiness of man shall be humbled, and the lofty pride of men shall be brought low, and the Lord alone will be exalted in that day. And the idols shall utterly pass away" (Isa. 2:17–18).

2. David Peterson, *Engaging with God: A Biblical Theology of Worship* (Downers Grove, IL: InterVarsity, 1992), 20.

3. Graeme Goldsworthy, *According to Plan: The Unfolding Revelation of God in the Bible* (Downers Grove, IL: InterVarsity, 1991), 87.

Chapter 7: Community

1. Tim Chester and Steve Timmis, *Total Church: A Radical Reshaping around Gospel and Community* (Wheaton, IL: Crossway, 2008), 47, 50.

2. Dietrich Bonhoeffer, *Life Together* (San Francisco: HarperSanFrancisco, 1954), 23.

3. First Corinthians 11 surfaces the issue of mistreating the Lord's Table as an opportunity to eat and drink rather than to be community around the new covenant of Jesus.

4. This formula is one reason why community groups should constantly seek to multiply, to keep communication simple and intimate.

5. "And the Lord gave the people favor in the sight of the Egyptians" (Ex. 11:3).

6. Chester and Timmis, *Total Church*, 62.

7. Ibid., 57, 59.

Chapter 8: Community Distortions

1. Joseph H. Hellerman, *When the Church Was a Family: Recapturing Jesus' Vision for Authentic Christian Community* (Nashville: Broadman, 2009), 139.

2. Matt. 18:21–35 is good depiction of this element.

3. Lesslie Newbigin, *The Gospel in a Pluralistic Society* (Grand Rapids, MI: Eerdmans, 1989), 227.

4. Tim Chester and Steve Timmis, *Total Church: A Radical Reshaping around Gospel and Community* (Wheaton, IL: Crossway, 2008), 59.

5. Bruce A. Ware, *Father, Son, and Holy Spirit: Relationships, Roles, and Relevance* (Wheaton, IL: Crossway, 2005), 22.

Chapter 9: Mission

1. Andreas J. Köstenberger and Peter T. O'Brien, *Salvation to the Ends of the Earth: A Biblical Theology of Mission*, New Studies in Biblical Theology 11, ed. D. A. Carson (Downers Grove, IL: InterVarsity, 2001), 219.

2. For a brief, helpful discussion on human freedom, see chap. 3 in Bruce A. Ware's *God's Greater Glory: The Exalted God of Scripture and the Christian Faith* (Wheaton, IL: Crossway, 2004).

3. G. K. Beale, *The Temple and the Church's Mission: A Biblical Theology of the Dwelling Place of God*, New Studies in Biblical Theology 17, ed. D. A. Carson (Downers Grove, IL: InterVarsity, 2004), 402.

4. John Calvin, *Institutes of the Christian Religion*, trans. Henry Beveridge (Peabody, MA: Hendrickson, 2008), 1.5.1.

5. In *The Mission of God: Unlocking the Bible's Grand Narrative*, Christopher J. H. Wright explains, "The earth is the Lord's. The earth, then, belongs to God because God made it. At the very least this reminds us that if the earth is God's, it is not ours. We do not own this planet, even if our behavior tends to boast that we think we do. No, God is the earth's landlord and we are God's tenants. God has given the earth into our resident possession (Ps. 115:16), but we do not hold the title deed of ultimate ownership. So, as in any landlord-tenant relationship, God holds us accountable to himself for how we treat his property" (Downers Grove, IL: InterVarsity, 2006), 397.

6. "Only Christians, armed with the Word and Spirit, planning and working to spread the kingdom and righteousness of Christ, can transform a nation as well as a neighborhood as well as a broken heart." Timothy Keller, *Ministries of Mercy: The Call of the Jericho Road*, 2nd ed. (Phillipsburg, NJ: P&R, 1997), 26.

7. Wright, *The Mission of God*, 391–92.

Chapter 10: Mission Distortions

1. Timothy Keller, *Ministries of Mercy: The Call of the Jericho Road*, 2nd ed. (Phillipsburg, NJ: P&R, 1997), 54.

2. Christopher J. H. Wright, *The Mission of God: Unlocking the Bible's Grand Narrative* (Downers Grove, IL: InterVarsity, 2006), 452.

3. Tim Chester and Steve Timmis, *Total Church: A Radical Reshaping around Gospel and Community* (Wheaton, IL: Crossway, 2009), 178.

4. Taken from Walter C. Kaiser Jr., *Quest For Renewal: Personal Revival in the Old Testament* (Chicago: Moody, 1986).

Chapter 11: Plan

1. Timothy Z. Witmer, *The Shepherd Leader: Achieving Effective Leadership in Your Church* (Phillipsburg, NJ: P&R, 2010), n.p.

2. Jerry Bridges, *Respectable Sins: Confronting the Sins We Tolerate* (Colorado Springs, CO: NavPress, 2007).

Chapter 12: Multiplication

1. "And Jesus came and said to them, 'All authority in heaven and on earth has been given to me. Go therefore and make disciples of all nations'" (Matt. 28:18–19). "I do not ask for these only, but also for those who will believe in me through their word" (John 17:20).

2. "For the love of Christ controls us, because we have concluded this: that one has died for all, therefore all have died" (2 Cor. 5:14). "The aim of our charge is love that issues from a pure heart and a good conscience and a sincere faith" (1 Tim. 1:5).

3. Tim Chester and Steve Timmis, *Total Church: A Radical Reshaping around Gospel and Community* (Wheaton, IL: Crossway, 2008), 111.

4. Christopher J. H. Wright, *The Mission of God: Unlocking the Bible's Grand Narrative* (Downers Grove, IL: InterVarsity, 2006), 533.

GENERAL INDEX

Abraham, 123–24
abuse, 81–84
accountability, 109
anger, 77, 116–17, 181, 201
apologetics, 174–75, 179–81

Beale, Greg, 156
behavior modification, 46, 129,
 147, 173, 200
blessings, 69
Bonhoeffer, Dietrich, 31, 125
boundaries, 17–18
Bridges, Jerry, 201

Calvin, John, 124, 223
Chester, Tim, 135–36
Christian community, 71–72,
 84, 130–34, 141–50, 196–97
Christian maturity, 65–66
Christian witness, 134–37
codependency, 68
confession, 128–29, 198
conversion, 164
covenants, 96, 177
creation, 16–17, 20, 69–70,
 102, 156–60
creationists, 95

cultural engagement, 160–67
culture, 149–50

David, 123–24
death, 18–19
discernment, 48
discipleship, 53, 65–66, 185–
 217

early church, 124–25, 161
Edwards, Jonathan, 98, 124
entitlement, 46
evangelism, 93, 135–37,
 149–50, 171–72
evil, 27

failures, 76–78, 186–87
faith, 19
fear, 113–20, 186–87
felt needs, 141
final judgment, 33
forgiveness, 129, 198, 209–12
free will, 80–81, 154
freedom, 46–48

God, finding identity in, 75–87,
 113; glory of, 100–103, 108,

227

SCRIPTURE INDEX

RE:LIT

Resurgence Literature (Re:Lit) is a ministry of the Resurgence. At www.theResurgence.com you will find free theological resources in blog, audio, video, and print forms, along with information on forthcoming conferences, to help Christians contend for and contextualize Jesus's gospel. At www.ReLit.org you will also find the full lineup of Resurgence books for sale. The elders of Mars Hill Church have generously agreed to support Resurgence and the Acts 29 Church Planting Network in an effort to serve the entire church.

FOR MORE RESOURCES

Re:Lit – www.relit.org
Resurgence – www.theResurgence.com
Re:Train – www.retrain.org
Mars Hill Church – www.marshillchurch.org
Acts 29 – www.acts29network.org

Dan's employee Chris :-

Nake - School

Rob - vol.